GEORGIE & ELSA

NORMAN THOMAS DI GIOVANNI

Georgie & Elsa

Jorge Luis Borges and His Wife
The Untold Story

The Friday Project
An imprint of HarperCollinsPublishers
77–85 Fulham Palace Road
Hammersmith, London W6 8JB
www.harpercollins.co.uk

First published in Great Britain by The Friday Project in 2014
Copyright © Norman Thomas di Giovanni 2014
www.digiovanni.co.uk

1

Norman Thomas di Giovanni asserts the moral right to
be identified as the author of this work

A catalogue record for this book
is available from the British Library

ISBN 978-0-00-752437-2

Grateful acknowledgment is made to the Lilly Library for permission
to reproduce the photograph of the Colonel Suárez monument.

Designed and typset by Marcial Souto,
Barcelona and Buenos Aires

Printed and bound in Great Britain by
Clays Ltd, St Ives plc

To M., who guided and inspired
To Derek and to Tom

Contents

A note on Borges will be found following page 259

Prologue
A Figure of Speech

Synecdoche, a part standing for the whole.

In 1944, in the kind of incisive and highly literary statement typical of him, the celebrated Argentine poet and storyteller Jorge Luis Borges postulated in one of his tales that 'Any life, no matter how long or complex it may be, is made up essentially *of a single moment* – the moment in which a man finds out, once and for all, who he is.'

Borges's ultimate fame as a writer is based on a mere thirty-four stories written between 1933 and 1953 and published in two collections, *Ficciones* and *El Aleph*. His fiction was unpopular at the time, considered cryptic and abstruse, and it wasn't until he was in his seventies that he began to be swamped with awards and prizes and honours – among them, honorary degrees from both Oxford and Cambridge.

At birth he had been given his father's first name. In a household of English speakers – with a grandmother and great aunt of English stock – it was only natural that to distinguish father and son he be dubbed Little Jorge, or Georgie. The name stuck. To his family and to a handful of intimates he was known ever after as Georgie.

The story told here in *Georgie & Elsa*, in which I was both reluctant witness and tricky participant, took place in a three-year span between 1967 and 1970. What I have recounted, besides depicting and illuminating hitherto unknown facts and events in the couple's affairs, is an attempt to find out whether a person's life can be typified by a single part of it. Can the ups and downs and vicissitudes of a brief marriage reflect and define the essential character of either of the partners in that alliance? In short, can a marriage of only a few years' duration reveal a man's whole life? The man is Borges. What does his short, failed marital union with Elsa Astete Millán tell us about him?

1   Celebrating the Marriage

Jorge Luis Borges and Elsa Astete Millán were married at a Buenos Aires registry office on 4 August 1967. The occasion seems not to have excited the notice of the press. On 21 September came a follow-up ceremony in the Iglesia de Nuestra Señora de las Victorias, where both Borges's mother Leonor and his sister Norah – the two of a religious bent – had married.

These events took place on the eve of Borges's departure for Harvard University, where, over the following months, he was to deliver the prestigious Charles Eliot Norton lectures. Hitherto a life-long bachelor, Borges was sixty-eight years old at the time of the wedding; Elsa, a widow, with a son in his twenties, was eleven years younger. The trip to Cambridge she described as her honeymoon; as for the lectureship she appeared to look on it as an altogether secondary matter.

The church of their marriage had been built in 1880 in the plain neo-Gothic style of the time and place, the belltower and steeple, with its four pinnacles, towering over

the buildings crowded round it. Soon after, in 1883, the
edifice was given to the Congregation of the Redemptorists
on the day of their first arrival in Buenos Aires. Founded
in Italy in 1732, the Congregation is a missionary society
whose aim is to put into action Jesus Christ's command
to 'Love one another as I have loved you.' In 1884, the
Church of Our Lady of the Victories also became a seat of
the cult of Our Mother of Perpetual Help, the Byzantine
icon of which the Redemptorists are caretakers. Such was
the improbable and incongruous setting for the marriage
of a man of Borges's well-known agnosticism and sceptical
turn of mind.

In the published pictures of the church ceremony Borges
stood staring ahead, hands behind his back, with Elsa on
his right and his mother of ninety-one on his left. The church
was packed with friends and well-wishers, along with
numerous members of the press and their accompanying
photographers. The bride wore a black coat-dress, with a
pair of long black gloves, and a white turban-like hat with a
short, gauzy veil over thick false eyelashes. Neither Georgie
nor Elsa looked as if it were the happiest day of their lives.
While Leonor appeared solemn, the couple seemed glum.

According to Borges, on the day of their civil marriage
his mother told Elsa that to her only a church ceremony
counted. The gauntlet had been firmly thrown down at
Elsa's feet.

2 A History of the Romance

There is no definitive account of the romance – early, middle, or late – between Georgie and Elsa. Dates are absent or contradictory, and the resulting picture is full of gaps and distortions. There are her versions of events but little from Borges's side except for some brief remarks he once made to me about why he married her. (His explanation smacked at one and the same time as overly literary and foolishly romantic.)

Elsa recalled their initial meetings in a rosy and seemingly sincere way while she and Borges were married but after they separated her emphasis changed. She now glossed over those early days and spoke more of their life together. In her recollections of both times there are false notes and plain untruths, especially when she describes the latter years. Surprisingly, looking back on the marriage and her relationship with Borges in 1983, when she was seventy-two and Borges still had three years to live, she expressed neither bitterness nor resentment nor recriminations. In fact, she presented a blissful, storybook picture of their entire married life that had little to do with reality. For some unknown reason she was putting the best possible face on events that had not been pleasant for her.

So what we have is a series of fragments, many of them unreliable. In the maze and tangle of what really took place in the romance – somewhere – lies the irreducible truth. By now, however, that truth is elusive if not irretrievable.

The story begins, according to one Elsa version, which she recounts with girlish enthusiasm and hints of prophetic significance, when she was seventeen and Borges twenty-eight. That would have made it 1927. (Other accounts give their ages as twenty and thirty-one, but for a moment let's follow Elsa's lead.)

She grew up on the fringes of La Plata, then a pleasant university town and capital of the Province of Buenos Aires, an hour or so southeast of the city of Buenos Aires. The university was renowned for its distinguished faculty, its important library, and a celebrated Natural History Museum. Founded in 1882, La Plata was carefully laid out on a grid plan; it had intersecting diagonal avenues and it boasted impressive woodlands and parks and public buildings. Elsa remembered it sentimentally as 'a beautiful, never-to-be-forgotten city, fragrant with its lindens.'

She described herself at the time as *una jovencita vistosa* – an attractive young woman. One day she accepted an

invitation from Pedro Henríquez Ureña, an outstanding
scholar and literary figure, to have tea that afternoon at
his home. Some young writers from Buenos Aires had
also been invited, among them – fatefully – Borges. 'I say
fatefully', Elsa recounted, 'because I did not want to accept the invitation. I no doubt had another engagement,
which I did not want to break.' She arrived at Henríquez
Ureña's in a bad mood and took her good time about
entering the room where the others were gathered. She
claimed that from the time she was a small girl she had
been in the habit of not speaking when anything or any-
body displeased her. (She noted that the habit was one
she never lost.) So she took a seat in an armchair and did
not utter a word. Georgie stared at her, he too speechless.
Later he confessed to her that he had been terrified. She
claims to have found him a kind, talented, good-looking
young man. These last words were an obvious sop to
Borges, who was present when Elsa spoke them. If on
their first meeting both were tongue-tied, she could
hardly have judged his kindness or his literary talent. As
for his looks, Borges in the twenties was decidedly un-
prepossessing. At one point he wore thick spectacles that
greatly magnified his eyes, and his right eyelid drooped.
Later he began to put on weight and grew a beard. In all
these stages he was extremely awkward in the presence
of the opposite sex. Elsa had been upset on the day because she'd had to give up a date with some other man.

Yet if there is any truth to her stories something must have been in the air, for she mentions that many pleasant afternoons were to follow, both in La Plata and in Buenos Aires, and she names the different tea shops she and Borges frequented.

Another version of events states that Henríquez Ureña had invited Elsa and her sister Alicia on a sort of blind date to a lecture at the Museum of Fine Arts. The speaker turned out to be Néstor Ibarra, who was one day to marry Alicia. The young man who'd accompanied him to La Plata was Borges. Elsa is quoted as saying that 'after Henríquez Ureña introduced us we had tea at the Jockey Club, and the next week Alicia and I went to Buenos Aires, where we all met up. From then on Borges never left me alone. He pursued me night and day. It was on our first date that he swore his eternal love for me.'

For how long this went on we do not know. It has been claimed that they were sweethearts for two years and that there was even talk of marriage, but Elsa once remarked that she couldn't remember if they were ever formally engaged. Interviewed in 1983, she spoke of having been Borges's fiancée when she was twenty years old. 'We had even exchanged rings,' she said. 'We were properly engaged.'

Again, taking the lead from Elsa, let us now say she was twenty. That would have made Borges thirty-one and the year 1930. She claimed that a besotted Borges journeyed to La Plata every Saturday to see his beloved. But what the beloved never revealed to him was that she had fallen in love with someone else, with whom she was carrying on a clandestine relationship. Borges, incredibly callow, was the last person to find out. One variant of the story quotes Elsa as saying that 'A fortnight after I was married, Borges, who knew nothing about it, kept phoning my house. My mother did not know what to say to him, and I washed my hands of the matter. I told her it was her problem. Finally, being very correct, my mother answered one of his calls and said, "Look, Borges, pardon me, but I feel obliged to tell you something. Don't phone any more; Elsa is married."' The mother reported that there was a short silence down the telephone and then Borges said, '*Ah*, *caramba*,' and he hung up.

There is something amusing about this story, but it does Elsa no credit, while it makes an utter fool of Borges. Can things really have happened in this way? Was Elsa's memory plainly unreliable or was she simply good at invention? When would these events have taken place? We know that Elsa was not married until 1937. Several years are unaccounted for here.

While there is no full or straightforward account of the romance there is no end of inconsequential variations. In one, María Millán, Elsa's mother, ran a boarding house, where Borges stayed during his visits and where Henríquez Ureña was a lodger. It was here, not at the professor's home nor at the Museum of Fine Arts, that Elsa first met Borges.

One thing only seems certain – that this was Borges's first of several experiences of being deceived and jilted by a woman. What lesson did he derive from the Elsa misfortune?

In the whole fraught saga of his star-crossed relationship with Elsa, what happened next, early in 1944, must rank as one of the strangest turns in Borges's life. By this time Elsa had been married since 1937 to one Ricardo Albarracín Sarmiento, by whom she had a son. In this seven-year interim she and Borges are not known to have been in contact. Under what circumstances then and by what plotting did he meet Elsa again? All we know is what he wrote to her in two love letters, both composed in the same week. These mysterious billets-doux, giving no hint of a before or an after, seem to have materialized out of nowhere, led nowhere, and ended nowhere.

The first of these impassioned letters, written on 31 January, reveals that Georgie and Elsa had met the day before, an encounter that unleashed a veritable Niagara of emotion in the normally buttoned-up Borges. Apart from his amatory outpourings, he says he would like to overwhelm her with a detailed description of his room, with his bookcase containing the *Encyclopædia Britannica*, his shelves of Chesterton's works, and his various editions of the Arabian Nights. And he recommends that she read the anthology of fantastic literature that he had compiled a few years earlier with his friends Adolfo Bioy Casares and Silvina Ocampo.

In the second letter, written on 4 February, he tells Elsa that two days earlier he had gone to *Sur*, the leading literary magazine of the period, to correct the proofs of his latest short story and to add a dedication. The dedication was one he had obviously promised her when they met. Indeed when the issue of *Sur* appeared his tale bore the inscription 'To E.H.M.', initials standing for Elsa Helena Millán. The missive goes on to say that the Sunday editions of both Buenos Aires papers, *La Prensa* and *La Nación*, are reviewing a book of his poems. We learn that the following week he is going to 'undertake a pilgrimage to La Plata.' And he closes telling her that he is in the midst of correcting the final proofs of Sarmiento's nine-teenth-century classic *Recuerdos de provincia*, wherein her surname – that is, her husband's surname, Albarracín – appears countless times, as well as revising Spanish trans-lations of Carlyle and Emerson and completing 'a long metaphysical essay for *Sur*.'

So much for the letters' factual information. It is almost unbelievable that Borges would seek to impress or at-tempt to attract a young married woman with no literary interests whatsoever by reciting to her the contents of his library shelves or the trivia of his proofreading, editing, or writing activities. The dedication, yes, may have proved

momentarily flattering, but the rest in a man of forty-four
is more like the hopeful but clumsy groping and fumbling
of an adolescent.

More revealing are the overblown expressions of love.
'To have witnessed the birth and death of your slow smile,
to have heard the precious modulations of your voice, to
have recaptured for a few hours the intricate delight of your
company . . .' He then tells Elsa she is not just a miracle
but is also indispensable, and he begs her not to go out of
his life. On it goes; each bit of his soul-baring, each of his
declarations, more embarrassing than the last. 'Those who
suffer the misfortune of not being Helena Astete Millán
have no reality for me . . .'

What on earth could have provoked these pathetic
effusions – pleading with Elsa to deliver him from his
loneliness and the pointlessness of his existence, admitting
to a fear that while he remembers her he may no longer
exist in her memory? All so uncharacteristic of the Borges
he allowed the public to see.

For anyone else this isolated episode might have been a
simple aberration. But for Borges it was part of a recurring
pattern. As ever with him, we must look for an explanation in the ongoing frustrations and failures of his love
life, in the string of rejections he suffered at the successive
hands of women he fell in love with, or imagined he was
in love with, but who in time either spurned him outright
or strung him along or simply failed to respond to his

style of literary advances. Borges's love life was always a cerebral business.

What seems to have triggered the 1944 letters to Elsa was a reaction. Borges had endured a long-running obsession with Norah Lange, a captivating redhead, a poet whose first book he had assiduously promoted in 1925 and to whom he soon became romantically attached. She was Nordic, tall, good-looking, and with flaming hair – by his standards everything a woman should be. By 1931, however, Norah was conducting a secretive on-and-off affair with another poet, Oliverio Girondo. This was a blow to Borges, but when Oliverio departed for Paris, Borges's hopes began to wax again. Then, when his rival returned, the hopes – always a private intellectual exercise – once more waned. Norah and Oliverio lived together for nearly a decade and in June 1943 were quietly married. Meanwhile, Haydée Lange, Norah's sister, had an unstable boyfriend who was convinced that Borges was carrying on with his fiancée. He spied on Haydée, trying to catch Borges. At the end of 1943 the young man was found drowned in the harbour.

It was at this time that Borges's mind seemed to snap and he reacted by trying to revive his old relationship with Elsa. What we don't know is how the earlier connection with Elsa fit in chronologically with Borges's ongoing love of Norah Lange, which in fact he never got over.

Elsa, who was the most jealous of women, admitted in

her last years that Borges was always in love, that he needed
love ('even if perhaps this is not quite the right word for
it'), that he needed a woman by his side. When his feelings
for one were over, he soon found a replacement. 'But for
some unknown reason,' Elsa went on, 'he never managed
to make anything permanent with any woman.' Was she
being coy in this last remark or was it some sort of cryptic
cover-up?

With regard to the love letters of 1944, as mysteriously
and unexpectedly as the isolated episode had risen it simply
faded or went underground. There were no repercussions at
the time, and the event appeared to vanish from Borges's
life. When in 1944 he published in book form the story
dedicated with fanfare to Elsa twelve months before, oddly
the dedication was shifted to another of the collection's
stories, which was dated 1942. As for the fate of the two
letters, in 1986 Elsa unsuccessfully offered them for auc-
tion at Sothebys in New York, but the suggested price of
$4,000-6,000 had apparently been deemed by the public
as too high. Also oddly, when asked in 1983 whether
Borges ever dedicated a book to her, Elsa remembered a
book and a poem. She was wrong about the book, right
about the poem, but all memory of the story seemed to
have slipped her mind. The omission of the name Astete
from the dedication, by the way, may have been a nicety
on Borges's part. He once told me that Elsa hated the
name, since as a schoolgirl she had been teased for it by

the other children. In Spanish the last two syllables, *tete*, are close to meaning 'tit'.

The third and final phase of Borges's infatuation with Elsa is as fragmentary and hard to pin down as the first two. We have few hard facts or solid documentation, but reams of gossip and much partisan speculation by a parade of busybodies. Commentators and biographers, long after the event, have resorted to interviews with some of Borges's friends and members of his and his mother's social set. None of this gleaned information has been closely scrutinized or sifted for the truth. The recordists appear to have taken at face value whatever they were told. What has been recorded of Elsa's point of view is banal and evasive.

The question of who engineered the marriage – was it doña Leonor? was it Borges? – is still ambiguous. Doña Leonor swore to me that her son was adamant about marrying Elsa. Borges swore to me that his mother was adamant that he marry Elsa. His testimony must be questioned. Whenever Borges found himself in a tight or embarrassing corner he was notorious for exculpating himself and falling back on lies. The grossest example of this was the blame he laid on his mother for his marriage to Elsa.

In 1965, when he was offered the Harvard lectureship, a decision had to be made about who would accompany him to Massachusetts. His mother, who had previously

fulfilled the role of travelling companion, was approaching
her nineties. A suitable person was deemed necessary.
Up to this time Borges had been enjoying the company
of María Esther Vázquez, a young writer and journalist
nearly forty years his junior, who in 1964 had accompanied
him on a long meandering European journey. It is said
that on his return their relationship – as was inevitable
with Borges – had become closer, much to doña Leonor's
disapproval. She did not want to see him in the position
of Professor Rath with Lola-Lola of the Blue Angel. Any
younger woman, she feared, would take advantage of her
son; in short, Georgie needed someone older. María Esther
accompanied him to Peru early in 1965, but by this time
her intentions had been made clear. To Borges's distress
she had married the poet Horacio Armani. Once more
Georgie's romantic fortunes were repeating themselves.
(It is worth noting that several months after he and Elsa
married – this was at the time I first knew them in Cambridge – it was María Esther he often spoke to me about
with a poignant nostalgia when out of Elsa's earshot. He
also spoke to me this same way, but to a lesser extent, of
one of his students, Vlady Kociancich, on whom it was
plain to me that he had a crush.)

One version of Elsa's reappearance on the matrimonial
scene tells that Borges's mother learned that Elsa was now
a widow and urged her son to contact her. A meeting was
arranged via Elsa's sister Alicia. Elsa showed Borges a ring

he had given her years before; he was moved that she had kept it. Borges later showed Elsa a photograph of her that he had kept between the leaves of a book; doña Leonor told Elsa that for years he looked at it every night before going to bed. All this is too pat and smacks too much of a fairy tale to ring true.

Exactly when these events were supposed to be taking place we do not know. There was some mention of Elsa's qualifications, as she knew no English. A second version of the story is that another of Borges's old flames, Margarita Guerrero, was mooted as a possible wife. This too seems to me an absurdity. Margot, as she was known, was a striking beauty, tall, elegant, and worldly. All the things Elsa was not. Was Margot one more of Borges's – or his mother's – preposterous fancies?

Eventually Borges chose Elsa, proposed to her, and she accepted. Again there are no dates for any of this. Plans were made for the registry and the church ceremonies. Now it was time for Elsa – unknown in Buenos Aires literary or social circles – to be paraded for inspection. As was to be expected, doña Leonor's circle of upper-class women, snobs to the last one, sniffed and probed and found Elsa wanting. It was an ocular inquisition. She proved frumpish, unsophisticated, and lacking in looks. It is true that even with her mouth shut tight Elsa was loud. When she laughed her cackle turned shrill and went on far too long. But she would have had little to laugh about at these gatherings; Elsa knew what was taking place and in the end she got her own back by snubbing the lot of this smart set who had arranged a party for the newlyweds on the eve of their departure for the United States. Elsa simply did not show up, leaving Georgie to attend the gathering on his own.

Within a week the couple set off on their great adventure, arriving in Boston on 29 September 1967.

3   Off on the Wrong Foot

At Harvard, Elsa was immediately plunged into the thick of an academic community and a life that she could not have foreseen and that Georgie could not have prepared her for. This was not the froth of upper-class, pseudo-intellectual Buenos Aires ladies who had informed a large part of Borges's existence in Argentina. Elsa could deal with such people by ignoring them and falling back on her own family and friends.

Here in Cambridge, Borges's colleagues were all each other's close friends as well as being highly professional world-class Hispanic scholars. Borges had made the acquaintance of some of these men and women during a visit to Harvard with his mother in 1961 or 1962, when he spent a semester at the University of Texas. Others were old friends and associates from earlier years together in Buenos Aires.

Juan Marichal, who had been at Harvard since 1949, was chairman of the Romance Languages and Litera-tures Department at the time of Borges's appointment to the Norton lectureship. Recognized as one of the most important intellectuals of the Spanish diaspora following the civil war, Marichal was a historian, literary critic, and essayist. He spent ten years rescuing and assembling the scattered and suppressed works of Manuel Azaña, a leading politican and victim of the Franco dictatorship. Marichal's wife was Solita Salinas, daughter of the poet Pedro Salinas – whose writings Marichal also edited – and sister of the Madrid publisher Jaime Salinas.

It so happened that one of the late Pedro Salinas's closest friends and associates was Jorge Guillén, whom Borges regarded as the finest living poet of the Spanish language. In retirement, Guillén resided in Cambridge with his wife Irene and his daughter Teresa, who was married to Stephen Gilman, also a Harvard professor. Gilman was a Hispanist who wrote, among other books, specialist studies of classics like the Cid and the *Lazarillo de Tormes*, the theatre of Lope de Vega, the fifteenth-century *La Celestina*, its author Fernando de Rojas, and the nineteenth-century novelist Benito Pérez Galdós.

Between all these people the links were tight. To occupy his time and keep from falling into boredom, in addition to his six public lectures Borges in his first term at Harvard gave a small class on Argentine writers. Who was it who volunteered to pick him up from his flat and shepherd him to his classroom, where they sat in on his lectures? Teresa Gilman and Irene Guillén.

Also at Harvard was the unassuming Raimundo Lida, whom Borges had known since the early 1930s and the founding of *Sur*. Lida had then served as its managing editor. From 1953 he had been at Harvard, where he preceded Marichal as department chairman. Lida was a philologist, a philosopher of language, and an expert in the Romance philology of the Spanish Golden Age. He had been born into a Yiddish-speaking family in a part of the Austro-Hungarian empire that is now Ukraine. When only a few months old he emigrated with his family to Buenos Aires. His wife was Denah Lida, a professor at nearby Brandeis University, where her specialities were Ladino and Sephardic languages. She too wrote a book on Pérez Galdós. It was Lida who retrieved Borges and Elsa from the airport on their arrival and helped set them up in their first flat.

Joan Alonso, the widow of another scholar known to Borges, also formed part of the preceding circle. Amado Alonso had been born in Spain, but emigrated to Argentina before he finally established himself at Harvard. He had been a distinguished philologist, linguist, and literary critic. Joan, who was not of Spanish origin, had at some point become a friend of Borges's mother, with whom she carried on a correspondence and reported to doña Leonor on Borges and Elsa's comings and goings in Cambridge.

There was another Argentine well known to Borges who taught at Harvard at this time – the writer, literary critic, and novelist Enrique Anderson Imbert. His stories, branded *micro-cuentos*, were much admired in the Argentine at the time for their blend of fantasy and magical realism. Borges loathed and looked down on Anderson Imbert, partly from envy of the latter's success and partly because Borges disliked being linked to Anderson through the kind of writing they both exercised. Consequently at Cambridge they hardly ever met.

Such then was the company Elsa was expected to keep. It was not her lack of English that turned out to be the problem; all these people spoke Spanish. Rather, it was her lack of intellect. Borges, who should have foreseen this, was simply oblivious of the problem. As ever, he was locked in self-absorption, in his own private, hermetic existence. He made a feeble attempt to interest Elsa in English by applying to her one of his pet ideas – that of learning a language through the study of its poetry. He saddled her with a favourite text, Robert Louis Stevenson's brief 'Requiem':

Under the wide and starry sky
   Dig the grave and let me lie:
Glad did I live and gladly die,
   And I laid me down with a will.

This be the verse you 'grave for me:
   Here he lies where he long'd to be;
Home is the sailor, home from the sea,
   And the hunter home from the hill.

But Elsa had no interest in English verse; Borges should have known the experiment was doomed to fail.

On one occasion, as Borges told it, Elsa baulked and refused to attend a party given by some of his Harvard colleagues when she learned that her husband was not to be the guest of honour. But Elsa was cleverer than Borges gave her credit for. This was her way of extricating herself from a class of people she simply could not deal with, allowing her to escape from the real or fancied humiliation she felt in their company. Consequently, social engagements and invitations dried up, and out of forced loyalty to his wife Borges was stuck at home, having to settle for a kind of bleak exile.

4   The Norton Lectureship

As Elsa had announced, she was going to be in Cambridge on a honeymoon. She can't have known a thing about the Charles Eliot Norton Professorship in Poetry or about any of the previous incumbents of the chair.

The lectureship had been founded in 1925 in memory of Harvard's first fine arts professor, who taught the subject from 1874 to 1898. The term poetry was interpreted in the widest sense to include musicians, painters, sculptors, and architects as well as poets, scholars, and writers. The incumbents are in residence throughout their tenure and are expected to deliver at least six lectures.

The series was inaugurated in 1926-27 by the venerable classicist Gilbert Murray. Among subsequent figures have been T.S. Eliot, Robert Frost, Igor Stravinsky, Aaron Copland, E.E. Cummings (who called his talks 'nonlectures' and warned from the outset that 'I haven't the remotest intention of posing as a lecturer.'), Herbert Read, Edwin Muir, Ben Shahn, Jorge Guillén, Pier Luigi Nervi, and Cecil Day Lewis. The 1940-41 lectures were delivered by Pedro Henríquez Ureña, the man who first drew Georgie and Elsa together, but it is unlikely that anyone would have brought this to Elsa's attention.

Elsa found fault with the living quarters obtained for her by the university but soon located a flat to her liking in Concord Avenue. Borges had been provided with an office in Radcliffe's Hilles Library, which he seldom used, and was offered the services of a secretary, John Murchison, an Anglo-Argentine graduate student.

In his lectures, Borges sat behind a table, stiff and upright, always insisting on having a glass of water in front of him, which he would reach out to touch to make sure it was the right distance from his hand. He refused to begin without it but rarely had recourse to it. Being blind he used no papers or notes. He had a large round pocket watch attached by a chain to his left lapel and would start by lifting the dial right up to his eye. That much he could make out. He knew he had to speak, hopefully without referring to the watch again, for at least fifty minutes.

He always dressed in a grey suit of a decidedly out-of-date cut. His necktie, which he referred to as 'a trick tie', was one of those ready-made affairs that he could clip together himself under his collar and not have to bother to knot. His stiffness and his old-fashioned clothes lent him an air of formality that he would not have been aware of. At the same time, unable to see or gauge his audience, he exuded unworldliness, vulnerability, and perhaps a hint of pathos.

Everyone seemed to be aware that they were about to be addressed by a lone blind man. As he sat waiting while a technician tested and adjusted a microphone, Borges would cradle one of his hands in front of him into the palm of the other.

Then he would begin. His spoken English was very good. He might stutter occasionally out of nerves and he had a bit of a Scottish burr which required getting used to. He did not have a loud register and was not good at projecting his voice, but this only made people listen more attentively. Out of fear of missing a word, his audiences kept exceptionally quiet.

When his nerves settled he would toss out the odd crowd-pleaser so as to get his listeners to warm to him.'Of course, I'm decidedly old-fashioned,' he would say, and they would howl with delight. Here was a writer worshipped for being the last word in avant-garde and he was claiming just the opposite. He would mention and quote from writers nobody read any more – De Quincey, Wells, Stevenson, Chesterton – suddenly giving them, in his audience's view, a new allure, a new promise. His reading had stopped around 1930 and he knew little or nothing of contemporary writers. This was another aspect of his appealing old-fashionedness – he made the past new, revisitable, and alive again.

It was uncanny how his tricks worked. His talks were simple, quite personal, and peppered with anecdotes ('My memory carries me back to a certain evening some sixty years ago, to my father's library in Buenos Aires') and idiosyncrasies. He frequently went off on asides – etymologies were one of his favourites. On days when he felt unsure of himself or of his audience he laid on the self-deprecation and, tongue in cheek, would belittle his own literary creation, which he spoke of as 'my so-called work'. Self-effacement was another of his tools. When he spoke of his life in writing, he would add, 'or trying my hand at writing'. He was never relaxed behind his table, and the public saw this, which put them on his side.

He could charm with his bookishness and his harmless 'out-of-the-way learning', as he called it. He quoted Shakespeare or Keats or Wordsworth seemingly at will and would flatter his listeners with his undisguised partisanship. He relished speaking of 'Literature – that is, English literature.' He fascinated his audience with his keen interest in remote subjects like Old English and Old Norse.

At the same time, his talks were not without their flaws. He misquoted, sometimes over-indulged in the self-effacement department, and often jumped from one subject to another without providing adequate transitions. The public never noticed or seemed to care. They were in the presence of Borges.

The truth is that audiences flocked to his lectures. Whether at Harvard, or the Poetry Center of New York's YM-YWHA, or countless classrooms across America, or the lowliest ill-lit, draughty, dilapidated auditorium of lost towns of his native pampa, Borges always packed them in. So many unexpected listeners turned up for his inaugural Norton lecture that the venue had to be shifted from the Fogg Museum and across Harvard Yard to the Sanders Theatre in rambling Memorial Hall.

Borges's first talk at Harvard, entitled 'The Riddle of Poetry', was given on 24 October 1967. The series of six he called *This Craft of Verse*.

5 Meeting Borges and Setting Out with a Master

In the late autumn of 1967, while Borges was mentally preparing his third lecture and Georgie and Elsa were nursing their marital bliss, I innocently entered their lives.

It was all a matter of accidents, coincidences, and luck. I'd been reading bits of Latin American poets, got hooked on Borges, and decided to repair to Schoenhof's foreign bookshop, in Harvard Square, for a copy of his collected poems in Spanish. When the clerk handed me the book he casually announced that Borges would be speaking there at Harvard the next week. I had no inkling Borges might be anywhere but in his own country.

I was in Memorial Hall that next week – it was 15 November – to hear his second Norton Lecture, a talk on 'The Metaphor'. Borges's spoken English immediately struck me, as did his views on his chosen subject. A week passed, and I sat down and wrote to him. My letter said that I was interested in producing a volume of his poems in English translation along the lines of the fifty poems from Jorge Guillén's *Cántico* that I had published two years before. It was all a stab in the dark. I had no idea of the regard in which Borges held Guillén, nor had I any idea that Guillén's daughter Teresa and wife Irene were attending Borges's classes on Argentine writers.

Within a week I had a reply from John Murchison, Borges's Harvard secretary, to tell me that Borges was pleased with my suggestion and 'would be delighted to have you phone him at his home ...'

A few days later I phoned. A woman answered, it was Elsa, but as I was unused to Argentine Spanish I thought hers was an Italian voice. She seemed to be speaking Italian when she called out, 'Georgie'. This was my introduction to the accent and intonation of rapid-fire *porteño* Spanish.

Borges answered, I identified myself, and he was at once lively and interested. He spoke in a clipped voice, with an English accent, and asked me right off what edition of the poems I had. When I told him, he said, 'Well, that's not the latest.'

'Oh, dear.'

'That's of no consequence,' he said. 'I don't know if the new edition is even in print yet. I have added a few new poems – all short ones. I have them all memorized.'

Then he asked would I come today. What time? Six o'clock. He gave me the address and repeated the apartment number twice. Eagerly, he also asked me to bring some of the translations. I told him he had misunderstood; I hadn't any translations yet but would be commissioning them.

'Well, come and we'll talk,' he said, his enthusiasm undiminished.

It did not occur to me then that Borges would have asked Teresa Gilman, or perhaps even Guillén himself, about me. I know in their loyalty they would have given me a warm report. Elsa would have invested this train of events with prophetic significance, calling it fate. But predetermination is not one of my beliefs; what was taking place at breakneck speed I knew to be just dumb luck.

That evening, for a couple of hours, Borges and I sat at a wooden table opposite each other on the benches of the flat's old-fashioned built-in breakfast nook. We discussed the planned volume in general terms and then went over some specific lines in a couple of poems I had been tinkering with in English translation.

The present book – the story I am trying to tell here – is about Georgie and Elsa. I want it to be a book about two married people, one of whom happens only incidentally to be a famous writer. My interest is strictly in them, not in literary criticism. And yet it was the work that Borges and I were embarking on that was the glue that held the three of us together. Perhaps, then – as an aside – the briefest, pedantry-free description of our daily enterprise would not be out of place.

I first read through his poems – they dated from 1923 to 1967 – and then joined him to hammer out a suitable broad selection. I brought notes, and while Borges would volunteer information about this or that poem I would scribble down jottings that might later prove useful to a prospective translator. Our views of what to include or exclude in a volume of a hundred poems rarely failed to coincide. Next I would take to our meetings a literal line-by-line handwritten draft of the poems, each of which we discussed at length. As Borges was blind, I read him one line at a time and added changes and corrections as he guided me.

There was a long history of visual abnormalities running through the male side of Borges's family. His father before him had lost his sight, and from his early years Borges was severely myopic. His vision had gradually deteriorated down the years until around 1955, when he could no longer read. When I met him he was able to distinguish the colour yellow as a luminous patch and so had a preference for yellow neckties. This too left him in time. When our books were published he would hold the title page up close to his face and make out the large letters. I noticed that he saw outlines better in bright light, and that his psychological state was a factor as well. This blindness worked to the advantage of our translations, since everything had to be read to him and demanded his strict attention.

For the rest, the task was one of lengthy administrative duties. On my own I began to match up poems and trans-lators, beginning with some of the same poets who had assisted me in the Guillén volume. This time I included myself among the translators. I corresponded with each contributor, criticized their English versions when they came back to me (often toing and froing with them several times per poem), and generally kept my stable of writers working. When I felt a poem was finished, I read it to Borges for a final nod of approval.

Other administrative duties consisted of raising funds to pay the translators and, most important of all, finding a publisher. It was a whirlwind of activity. I first met Borges at his flat on 4 December 1967. Before that month was out I had landed my publisher, Seymour Lawrence, and Borges had written to his, Carlos Frías, in Buenos Aires – dictating the letter to me – to secure English-language rights. I was amused and flattered when in the letter he referred to me as 'the *onlie begetter* of this generous enterprise'. He quickly explained that Frías was also a professor of English literature, so the Shakespeare link would not be wasted on him.

Work on these selected poems began in Cambridge, Massachusetts, and they were three years in the making before being finished in Buenos Aires. The book was then a fourth year in production.

I have mentioned that in the months before I met him Borges had chosen – had been forced to choose – isolation as his daily lot. Worse than his isolation was his stark loneliness. No one came to visit, he told me, and after a while he asked if I could come to work with him on Sundays.

His empty Sundays seemed to him to yawn on for ever. I was puzzled by this – the crowds at his public lectures, the emptiness at home – but I did not press him for an explanation. In the flat there was great tension between him and Elsa, which I feigned not to notice. I could see that he was immediately cheered by our work together, and he told me it gave him justification for his existence.

I said he told me that no one came to see him, but I remember that for a couple of days during my early visits a black boy, who may have been a Harvard student with an interest in writing, would be sitting in the kitchen with Borges. The young man said nothing, and Borges said nothing to him. I felt that Borges wanted to get rid of him by maintaining silence and not responding. As Borges snubbed him, the lad stopped coming. Borges never mentioned the incident nor did I.

Fani, the Borges's Argentine maidservant, reported that one day in Buenos Aires Borges received a visit from two Brazilian women. 'They stayed the whole afternoon,' Fani said. 'When they left the señor came to the kitchen and asked me what they were like physically. I told him they were blacks. "What do you mean blacks? Why didn't you tell me? ¡*Qué horror*, I would have thrown them out!"'

I don't know what it was about black people, but he did have an aversion to them. He sometimes wrinkled his nose and spoke of their *catinga*, an Argentine word for the smell of their sweat.

For her part, Elsa too seemed pleased to welcome me into the fold. I lifted her out of her gloom. My presence gave her more time for herself, needed space from Borges, and some new company she could trust.

6 Georgie's Mystery, Elsa's Bombshell

It was inevitable that Borges would begin to confide in me. There was no one else around with whom to converse, and talking to a stranger is always easier.

One day, when Elsa was out, he broke off from our work to tell me a story. He seemed troubled and confused, and his voice quickly took on a genuine sadness. Some weeks before, he and Elsa had been introduced to a John Van Dell and his wife, a couple living in Salem, Massachusetts. The Van Dells were former Argentines. Borges told me they were congenial people, and he and Elsa had enjoyed several pleasant occasions in their company.

The Van Dells would drive to Cambridge, pick up Georgie and Elsa, and take them touring Salem and other North Shore towns of interest. Of course to Borges Salem meant Nathaniel Hawthorne, the town's native son and one of his favourite American authors. Knowing this, Van Dell at once took Georgie and Elsa to visit the house of the seven gables.

The couples enjoyed several other outings together,

including meals at the Van Dells'. And then, suddenly, abruptly, and without explanation, there were no more meetings. In his puzzlement, Borges quizzed me for a possible reason for such a turn of events. There was obviously some key factor involved about which Borges was being kept in the dark, but I could not put my finger on it. Borges wanted to know if this were typical American behaviour. Quite untypical, I assured him, and with nothing more to offer, we let the subject drop.

Sometime during the university Christmas break Georgie and Elsa changed flats. They moved from the Concord Avenue entrance of their building just around the corner, where they could enter from the Craigie Street side. How Borges delighted to tell people they lived at Concord and Craigie, as if the words held some magical quality for him. He even worked the word Craigie into a new poem and launched into the root of the word.

Why the move at this time? What was the necessity of it? Maybe because Elsa was soon expecting guests – her son and later her cousin Olga – and she would have seen that more room was needed. But perhaps there was another contributing factor.

Along the corridor from the flat they vacated lived a Persian couple, as Borges referred to them. The man was a mathematician who had a theory of spherical time that fascinated Borges, although he did not understand it. Borges was also fascinated by the man's wife, to whom he frequently paid visits. She was a sultry beauty and, I think, a scholar herself. Obviously this did not go down well with Elsa, and she and Georgie had spats about it.

I found it odd that in his confidences to me about Elsa Borges always belittled and made fun of her. He would give a little laugh so that his words fell short of outright nastiness. She had been a schoolteacher, he once told me, bemused, and yet she would ask why they spoke Spanish and why were they Argentines. He said with a sneer that she enjoyed the company of members of Greater Boston's Argentine community, common people, non-scholars, non-intellectuals, with whom she could be her unfettered self. She went to their barbecues, where she stuffed herself on sweetbreads so that she would be laid up with a liver or pancreas attack for a day or two after. Taking to bed, she would have to lie on one side and drink lemon or grapefruit juice. Indeed, she had reported this behaviour to me herself, not without a touch of pride in her mischievous flirting with danger.

At the time I thought Borges's revelations showed unwarranted disloyalty to a new wife but I was too immersed in our work to look for any deeper meaning to any of this. The two had actually come to blows, he told me one day, and he illustrated his words by pummelling me on the back, gentler of course than she had done with him.

Just before Christmas Murchison informed me that Borges had moved out of the marital home and was holed up in Room 319 of the nearby Continental Hotel. I would have to meet him there. Borges explained to me that he'd had a tiff with Elsa and would be at the hotel for a few days. 'Tiff' was the actual word he used, and his usage somehow amused me.

Elsa, on another occasion, cornered me in the flat while I was waiting for Borges to wake from his customary after-lunch nap. In an angry, unprovoked tirade she confided that since they were first married Georgie had failed her as a man. I knew the two slept in separate rooms but had given this no special thought. Elsa had always struck me as a sexual animal but standoffish Borges never.

She obviously felt cheated. Georgie was impotent and always had been, she said. Why hadn't he told her from the start? He had waited until their wedding night, then thrown himself down on his knees before her, weeping. If only he had explained the situation beforehand, she seethed, adding bitterly, 'I know how to take a man to bed.'

Utterly stunned, I offered not a single word in reply. Elsa's frustration, her anger, her humiliation, her unhappiness, were now clear to me. So were Georgie's unhappiness and his secret burden.

7 A Visitor and a Yard of Ale

Ricardo, Elsa's son, arrived at the very end of December and stayed for one month, not the seven months his mother later claimed in the doctored memories of her 1983 interview. Nor did the young man and Borges spend a lot of time together, as Elsa claimed, on long, long Cambridge walks. Her memories were a fiction. In fact, the day before Ricardo's arrival it snowed all day, and the snow was deep and impassable on foot. A week later there were daylong sub-zero temperatures that Borges could not manage.

Before the cold weather set in, Borges had been going on and on about how much he looked forward to winter, for he hated the heat of Buenos Aires. Well, winter came, and it was a hard one. The pavements were icy and you had to shuffle along, skating gingerly, one foot in front of the other. His walking stick was of little use to him. He would hang on to my arm or to Murchison's for dear life. If he fell hard it might result in damage to his retina and the little he could see would be lost.

It snowed and it snowed. The mounds along the kerbs of

Concord Avenue grew higher and higher. Whenever the temperature dropped and the wind blew, walking anywhere became an ordeal. It was not long before Borges gave up going to his office at the Hilles Library. He was seeing and feeling at first hand what he came to call an 'epic winter'.

Twenty-six-year-old Ricardo was introduced to me as a Buenos Aires theatre director. Was this another fiction? He did once in my hearing discuss the personality and fate of Hamlet with Borges, but I kept getting glimpses of another side of him.

In the middle of January, Rita Guibert, an Argentine journalist living in New York, came to Cambridge to work on a lengthy interview with Borges for *Life en español*. She was accompanied by a photographer who trekked through the snow to shadow Borges and his students at the Hilles Library and to record him and Elsa in their flat. Ricardo appears in two of the Hilles photos, both times in close proximity to the most glamorous girl in the class. (Elsa and Murchison appear in one of these pictures, at a meal, she wearing sunglasses.)

Ricardo, a good-looking fellow, wore his hair slicked straight back and dressed in a V-neck sweater over a shirt with the sleeves of the former pulled back to his elbows. Elsa doted on him and regarded him proudly as a bit of a rake. He was married, of course, but I suspect he was separated from his wife. He quite soon struck me as a louche character and something of a spiv. When the pretty girl

retired to her Connecticut home for the term break Ricardo
prevailed upon me to help him with a love letter to her.

It was Borges who circulated the story that all Ricardo
and Elsa spoke about at the table during lunch, at afternoon
tea, and at supper was which streets of the city the No. 48
bus traversed on its long route out to Flores. Maybe
mother and son held such a conversation once. So what?
In his remarks about this, Borges, who was incapable of
inane talk, was airing his superiority. This was the kind of
denigrating anecdote, usually apocryphal, that he regarded
as clever and that he was constantly inventing to put
someone down.

I don't believe Borges ever took a shine to Ricardo but
he seemed to tolerate him for Elsa's sake and for the peace
and stability her son brought to the troubled household.

Just after the new year Borges was invited to a dinner
party given by Vail Read at her North Shore home in
Manchester, Massachusetts. Mrs Gardner Read, to be more
formal, was an official at Boston's Pan American Society
of New England. The party, a fairly large affair, was one
Borges did not want Elsa to attend, so he asked me to
accompany him instead.

Something odd and yet typical of the perverse whims
Borges was capable of took place in the car when we were
picked up. He sat beside the driver. I was in the back
alongside a young man who happened to mention that his
grandfather had been the leading Colombian Modernist

poet Guillermo Valencia. A few weeks before I had casually asked Borges about this poet and got a flat reply that he knew nothing about him. Now, suddenly, having overheard the conversation in the back seat, Borges began reciting one of the grandfather's most famous poems. I could not fathom it and never asked him for an explanation of the strange contradiction.

At the Reads' we met, among many others, Herbert Kenny of the *Boston Globe* and John Updike. I seized the opportunity to ask Updike to make some translations for me and he agreed. Across the table, Borges and Updike swapped the names of detective-story writers each had read. The list, which was encyclopedic, held the rest of us in thrall. It was almost as if the one was trying to outdo the other, but in a cheerful, non-competitive way.

It may also have been here at the Reads' table, if I remember correctly, that Borges and I invented – or, rather, first made public use of – the Old Norse. Whenever we were in company and Borges required the loo he would quietly say, 'Di Giovanni, do you think an Old Norse?' I would rise and, having reconnoitred the place beforehand, lead him straight to the bathroom and stand beside him to help point him and his stream in the right direction. Our code had originated when Borges first began to say to me that he thought it may be time for that old English custom, by which he meant taking a piss. But as I knew he had left the study of Old English behind and was now working on Old Norse I leapt at the play on words and contradicted him, saying, 'You mean an Old Norse, don't you?' After that, Old Norse stuck.

During this period Borges and I spent several evenings and nights together working late and then going out for dinner. I owned a VW Beetle, and Borges loved the occasional escape from the flat. One night he asked if we could go to a bar and drink some beer. To amuse him I took him to a place that specialized in something called 'a yard of ale'.

The yard of ale was drunk from what amounted to a long glass tube with a bulb at the end. You had to learn to lift the tube gradually and sip. If you tipped the tube up too quickly the whole yard rushed down to drench you. Somehow we mastered it and Borges was grinning like a naughty schoolboy. Afterwards, we took a drive down the Esplanade along the Charles on the Boston side of the river. We didn't get back to Craigie until midnight.

One of Borges's most popular poems is called 'El otro tigre' – the other tiger. At our destination I helped him to the little used Craigie Street entrance. From there he usually made his way up the one or two flights to the door of his flat. On this particular night, Borges could not wait to get upstairs to the loo. As soon as we entered the ground-floor door, he rushed under the stairway and opened his fly. He let go with an almighty flow and splash of piss that echoed loudly in the empty stairwell.

'Borges,' I said, pretending to be scandalized, 'what are you doing?'

'That's all right,' he said, 'they'll think it was some cat.'

'Sure,' said I, his mini-Niagara still reverberating in my ears, *'el otro tigre.'*

8 Vietnam, Olga, and Harvard Square

Neither Georgie nor Elsa had any idea of what was going on in the United States during the months of their visit. Borges could not read newspapers or did not have them read to him, did not listen to the radio, and would have found that discussing political issues with anyone – or having anyone discuss political issues with him – was too boring for his consideration.

One day a young reporter for the Harvard student paper, the *Advocate*, appeared at the flat to conduct an interview. He touched on all the literary bases and at some point asked Borges what he thought about the Vietnam war. Borges briefly expressed himself in favour of the war – that is, of the role of the United States in that war.

After the reporter left, I asked Borges what he knew about the war. He could not answer. I asked him on what basis he had come out backing American government policy. I then explained to him that the country was nearly engaged in a civil war over Vietnam, that university campuses were in turmoil about it, and that all of his colleagues – writers and intellectuals – were protesting daily and marching on Washington to express their opposition.

He went silent, then said, 'Well, di Giovanni, I thought Poe, Emerson, Whitman . . .'

On this flimsy literary basis he felt the United States could do no wrong. 'Yes,' I said, 'Poe, Emerson, Whitman – and then who, Borges? Lyndon Johnson?'

I had more than hinted that he should not speak, especially to reporters, about matters of which he knew nothing. I phoned the *Advocate* and had a cordial word with the interviewer. I asked if he thought it was fair to put questions to Borges about the Vietnam war. He agreed it wasn't and promised not to run Borges's statement. And he didn't.

This was the first of many times I was to stick my head above the parapet for Georgie. It was also the first time I was exposed to his blind political views.

The next guest to arrive at the Craigie Street flat was Elsa's cousin Olga. It was a mark of Elsa's ever increasing despair that as soon as her son had returned to Buenos Aires she required the familiar company of someone else who was close to her.

And Olga was close. Except in looks, Olga and Elsa were cut out of the same cloth. Now, in her cousin's company, Elsa had no need to keep up her guard. The cousin was so ingenuous, so naturally candid, that she would not have known what it meant to keep up one's guard. I liked that about Olga. She was incapable of putting on airs. She was just herself.

The two of them chittered and chattered incessantly, like a pair of cage birds. The way they spoke to each other fascinated me. Olga's word in agreement with anything Elsa said was '*lógico*', by which she simply meant 'of course'. In addition to this usage, the word 'logical' held another meaning for Elsa. She prided herself in being logical, by which she meant practical, down to earth, and it was always in contrast to Georgie, who was impractical, a dreamer.

Once, when the subject of Ricardo's wife came up, Elsa said, 'Tell di Giovanni, Olga, isn't Ricardo's wife divine?' To which Olga came back, 'Oh, yes, di Giovanni, Ricardo's wife is *divina – divina, divina, divina.*'

Yes, I told myself, so *divina* that her poor long-suffering husband is a confirmed womanizer.

There was something incorrigibly brazen about Olga.

I liked the way she spoke to Borges, without deference, as though he were part of the furniture, an old childhood friend, one of the family, which of course he now was. No one else knew how to speak to him in this straightforward manner. I liked the completely unselfconscious way she expressed herself with her body.

Olga was slightly shorter than Elsa. She wore loud combinations of clothes. On her, colours clashed, so that there was something of an out-of-tune brass band about her. Maybe it was her hair. The words 'peroxide blonde' had obviously been invented specially to describe its particular brash, strawlike colour. Apart from her earrings, necklaces, bracelets, and rings, Olga was adorned with the suntan of a New York widow who had long since taken up residence in Miami Beach.

And yet and yet . . . she was kindly and good-natured and I was truly grateful for the comic relief she unwittingly provided. Not for the others, perhaps, but certainly for me. I know that Elsa welcomed her; so did I. She was a waft of fresh air in a breathless, claustrophobic household.

The cousins were for ever off on shopping sprees, spending hours roaming Harvard Square together and gushing non-stop when they got back about the merits of this or that perfume, lipstick, eye shadow, false lashes, mascara, face cream, shampoo, hair conditioner. Georgie and I were always delighted to be left alone to get on with our work. In the late afternoon, exhausted and excited, the two piled in with their bags and tipped out the goodies. Then they could not rush fast enough to make us coffee. The only trouble with all this – at least from Borges's point of view – was that Olga would not have won prizes for her looks.

The women's outings brought them within range of a new species of local fauna – hippies. How the word tumbled off Olga's tongue. She had come from Argentina with hippies as the number one attraction that she wanted to see at Harvard. She was awestruck and could not hold back from asking was it true the odd ways they wore their hair?

The strange clothes they paraded about in? Was it true they smoked marijuana in public? I knew what was coming.

One day Elsa said, 'Di Giovanni, why don't you take Olga out some evening? She'd like to see some of the bars around Harvard Square.'

I did not know Olga to be a drinker. What she wanted was to be suitably chaperoned so that she could take in the sights in a discreet manner. Olga presenting herself discreetly. That was going to take some doing.

The appointed night came round, the two of us went out, and I must say that seeing the kick Olga got from our excursion was a genuine pleasure. She drank in the bright lights along the throbbing streets. She held tightly to my arm and asked an unceasing stream of questions and also kept pointing out for my inspection this or that person. Was it true that at home they slept on mattresses on the floor? Was it true that they exchanged partners for sex? Were they smoking pot?

It was hard to offer Olga a drink. I wondered whether she thought it might be spiked. She knew that speaking Spanish gave her a certain cover. Not even her scorched peroxide locks stood out in this crowd.

She did not insist in staying out very late. She couldn't wait to get back to Elsa so that she could tell all. Did Olga know that I was expressing my thanks to her for having come from afar to enliven the otherwise gloomy atmosphere of the Craigie Street flat?

9   Borges on Tour

Our work began to be noticed. The roster of poets who were engaged on our project were spreading the word. One whose ears that word reached was Galen Williams of the Poetry Center of the YM-YWHA, in New York, who had been badgered by the poet Alan Dugan to contact me for a proposed reading in April. She did and hired Borges, Murchison, and me on the spot.

Meanwhile, Murchison initiated our first reading, a trial run, at the Harvard Faculty Club. In preparation, he and I met at the Hilles Library, where he read aloud our choice of poems and I timed him. Our format was for me to recite the poems in English, Murchison in Spanish, and after each one for Borges to speak a couple of minutes, making impromptu remarks. That small inaugural reading went 'swimmingly', to use Borges's word for it.

An invitation soon followed for a reading at Brandeis University. There, when Borges sensed the packed house, he panicked. Gripping me by the arm he asked me to take him to the loo and, as we stood side by side watering the walls of the big white urinal in front of us, he begged me to get him out of this. I could scarcely believe it. Here was the professional who was delivering the prestigious, high-powered Norton lectures and suddenly he was caving in before my very eyes. Really, I was the one with the butterflies. This was the first time in my life I had performed in public on this scale. And it was to be alongside the illustrious Borges.

I knew I somehow had to take over and prop him up, ignoring the butterflies, his and mine, and simply assuring him it was going to be all right. Of course once we got started it proved more than all right. The audience loved what we were doing.

Since Borges was hard of hearing in his left ear, I sat to his right, with him in the middle and Murchison on his left. This way, after each of his contributions, I could lean towards him and with a whisper guide his performances, saying either 'Too long', 'Too short', or 'Just right.' Remarkably, I was later reputed to have ice-water in my veins when I read. Needless to say, Elsa chose not to attend any of these local outings.

Within days of Ricardo's departure Georgie and Elsa also departed. Their first stop was Smith College, then Princeton, then the University of Pennsylvania. They were back in Cambridge for less than a week before they were off again to Vassar. At some point there was – or had been – a brief tour of a couple of Texas universities. These visits took place before Olga's arrival. Borges was bored with Cambridge and he was slipping out of favour with his Harvard colleagues. These outside lectures gave him a taste of fresh blood and a degree of escape from Elsa's stranglehold. Paradoxically, it gave her an escape too.

It seems, however, that Marichal's feathers were ruffled by the amount of time Borges was travelling to lecture at other universities. Under the terms of the Norton lectureship he was meant to reside in Cambridge.

It was at this time, I suppose, seeing his popularity on other campuses and as well in retaliation or revenge for imagined slights, that Elsa began to taunt Georgie, telling him that this was his quarter hour of fame and that he must take advantage of the moment. By this she probably meant he should quickly hike up his lecture fees. Tomorrow, she would say, nobody will remember who you were. These remarks incensed Borges and he would repeat them to me with surprising frequency and irritation.

Although she had shown no interest in our previous readings, Elsa was not going to miss a chance to visit New York. There was one rub. Borges was adamant and pitiless about Olga's accompanying us. He flatly would not have it. Elsa begged me to plead with Borges to get him to relent. I felt sorry for Olga. Somehow I managed to get Georgie to agree to Elsa's request, but there was an iron-clad proviso. Olga had to stay at another hotel and was not to be seen with us.

Galen Williams made it quite clear that the reading at

the Y had to go like clockwork. The programme was to last an hour and a half, with one intermission, and everything had to end at a precise moment or else the Y would be in trouble with the unions. Of course Murchison and I had timed the poems and estimated Borges's contributions to the last second. Jack was one of the readers, I was another, and so were two of our poet-translators, Alan Dugan and Mark Strand. All of us, except for Borges, read from lecterns.

The Theresa L. Kaufmann Concert Hall, where the performance was taking place, was immense. From the stage you seemed to be looking out over an endless prairie. More daunting was the audience. It was packed with Borges connoisseurs, writers and poets, editors and publishers – the elite of the New York literary world.

At the end there was a tremendous ovation. Borges was relieved and elated, so elated that he called Elsa up onto the stage and had her recite one of his sonnets that she had memorized. The audience erupted in applause. Elsa could not have been more pleased.

Then suddenly from below the stage I was staring down into the face of Willis Barnstone, a poet and professor and great admirer of Borges. He was desperate to climb up beside us, wanting to read translations of his own of early Borges poems. He pleaded with me to stop the proceedings – that is, the public's exit from the auditorium – and grant him the podium. The request was not only beyond my power to grant, but it seemed such an absurd and amateurish thing to do.

Incredible how people who should have known better were desperate to bask in Borges's limelight. Elsa's recitation had been enough; the public liked it, but I felt Barnstone could have turned the evening into a vulgar circus. Months earlier, before Dugan had persuaded Galen to hire me, Barnstone had proposed to include in the reading a disproportionate seventeen of Borges's earliest poems, which dated from 1923. Georgie had been outraged that Barnstone was prepared to overlook his far better work of recent years.

The Barnstone fiasco did not end there. Galen had to write him a conciliatory letter the day after the reading. In it she said that I had actually listed him as reader for a first encore. She pointed out that

> We had fully expected that there would be at least one, if not three encores; but the drama of the evening was too much for encores. Once Borges had left the stage, it would have been awkward, anti-climactic, and unprofessional-amateurish. This evening shows that poetry can be 'show business' – a performance – and that the unexpected occurrences of the stage have to be 'expected.' For instance, who would have ever predicted that Borges would want his wife to read a poem and to sit on stage with him? It is unheard of in Poetry Center history, yet it worked beautifully!

Galen got an instant apology from Barnstone and there the matter rested. But at the same time she wrote to me saying that 'WB is, I've concluded, disorganized, paranoic and selfish!'

That night, after the reading, there was a cocktail party at Rita Guibert's. Two days later I returned to Cambridge with Borges. Mysteriously we lost, or contrived to lose, Elsa and Olga at Logan airport and ended up at an old North End haunt of mine, an Italian restaurant called Stella's. There we were meeting for lunch two *Atlantic* editors, Ann Holmes and Phoebe Adams. In the company of these two attractive women, Borges opened up like a sun-kissed blossom. He was particularly enjoying the naughtiness of the occasion. Mum was the word, as he was fond of putting his little secrets.

10   Invitations and Goodbyes

I wanted to try an experiment to see if the way Borges and I were going about our poetry translations could also be applied to his prose. I wrote out a rough draft of one of his stories, 'The Other Death', then sat down with him and went over it. I read him half a line of the Spanish followed by half a line of my English version. At once we saw the plan worked.

I confess that this involved way of making our translations – both the poetry and the prose – proved the most inefficient and time-consuming possible. But our interest – whatever it took – was in giving our work a painstaking linguistic accuracy that we found absent from most earlier translations of Borges's stories. We also wished to endow our English versions with the true colour of Borges's voice.

When 'The Other Death' was completed, I sent it to *The New Yorker*. They accepted it and asked us to call on them when we were in New York for the Y reading. They wanted to discuss offering us a contract.

As if this were not heady enough, around this same time Borges made me a pretty little speech. He had obviously been thinking it over, for his words came out with great formality. 'You have been very kind in showing me hospitality in your country,' he said. 'Now I'd like to invite you to Argentina and do the same for you in mine.'

I couldn't answer at once. When I did I said, 'Well, Borges, Argentina is not exactly just around the corner. I would not want to come as a tourist, but if we could find some work to do together ...'

'I think we can turn up something,' he assured me.

At the flat one afternoon when I appeared for my usual four o'clock work session, I found the entrance door ajar. I stuck my head in and called out. Suddenly, from a day-bed in one corner of the room, a blanket flew up and onto the floor sprang Elsa and Olga, startled. Elsa told me I was not to mention to Georgie what I'd seen. What had I seen? Nothing. The incident seemed entirely insignificant, and if Elsa hadn't told me not to say anything to Borges I would never have remembered it.

With her time in Cambridge drawing to an end, Elsa made herself busy with a number of last minute tasks. One, which she got me to do for her, was to go to the bank with a fistful of the dollars she had been collecting for Georgie's lectures and have them converted into $1,000 bills. I brought her back four, each with President Grover Cleveland's portrait on it. I could foresee that she was planning to impress her bank clerk in Buenos Aires when she handed them over the counter. Such was her mentality.

When the ordeal, the tension, of the reading at the Y was well over, I could turn my mind to our meeting earlier in the day with William Shawn and Robert Henderson of *The New Yorker* magazine. They offered and explained their generous contract, we accepted, and when they asked how the money should be split between us Borges lost not a beat in declaring fifty-fifty. When he and I had started out he'd asked about my money arrangement with Guillén. When I said half and half Borges's response stunned me. 'Is that enough for you?' he said. 'Perhaps you should take more.'

He gave his last Norton lecture two days later. It was titled 'A Poet's Creed'. Events concluded with a reception at the Signet Club, which Updike and his wife attended. I don't remember Elsa's being there. Murchison and I accompanied Borges back to the flat.

On 11 April 1968, to Elsa's visible relief, she and Georgie boarded a plane to Buenos Aires. Jack Murchison and I first took them to lunch along with Nina Ingrao, an Argentine friend of Elsa's, who had lent the couple furniture and furnishings for their flat. My memory is dim about when Olga went back. Jack and I drove Elsa and Borges to the airport and the next day returned to Craigie Street to close the place up.

11　Interregnum

Borges's last act at the airport, as we parted, was to hand me his walking stick as a gift.

Six full and fraught months were to pass before I saw Georgie and Elsa again. To earn money I took a job as a navvy planting shrubs on landscape construction sites. I did not let this impede the progress of my translations or editing. In my lunch breaks I sat scribbling away hunched over the steering wheel of a pickup truck. Evenings and weekends I got out dozens of letters to the poet-translators. My chief concern, however, was to keep up close contact and continuity with the Borgeses and with Murchison.

There were problems getting started. I did not trust my written Spanish so wrote letters to Borges in English and sent them to his mother, whom I expected would read them to her son and even answer them for him. As I should have foreseen, this did not go down well with Elsa, who soon admonished me. She said (20 June 1968) that she could take no responsibility for any post that was not sent *directly* (her italics) to their flat in Avenida Belgrano.

'Georgie,' she emphasized, 'no longer lives in Calle Maipú.' And she further pointed out that 'Unfortunately, Leonor is very old now and has lost some of her former capacity.'

This told me that there was friction if not rivalry between Elsa and her mother-in-law and not the harmonious relationship she had been leading people to believe. Elsa closed this letter telling me how busy she was arranging the house and that, together with the furniture, her and Georgie's much longed-for happiness had arrived. 'I do not want to recall the anguished days I lived [in Cambridge]', she went on; 'they were a costly price for the new, bright lives we are living now.'

Things did not rest there. The very next day Elsa wrote to me again to say that three days earlier Leonor had received a letter from me. 'I'm sorry for what is going on but I can't be helpful unless your post comes to this house . . . I must tell you once more that Leonor is very old and forgetful and Georgie is still as absent-minded as ever.' Then, still haunted by her experiences in Massachusetts, she remarked that wonderful Argentina brought her happiness. 'Doesn't it seem strange to you that I should speak of "happiness" now after having been so terribly unhappy [at Harvard]?'

After our initial hiccups about the post, Elsa and I exchanged numerous long, detailed letters, hers handwritten, mine typed. First to be dealt with were the ongoing minutiae that concerned the Craigie flat, the winding up of which was more or less tacitly left to Murchison and me.

By the end of April new tenants were in the apartment, but I still had two irons and a hair curler that belonged to the Spanish Department riding around in the back of my Volkswagen. Even towards the last week of October, Borges, via Elsa, was asking me to look into the business of getting their deposit on the flat returned.

I was also anxious to keep Borges informed of my dealings on his behalf with *The New Yorker* and with at least two book publishers who were in pursuit of us. Before Borges had left Cambridge I'd stuck my neck out and told him that his unceasing production of sonnets, all with their same line lengths and repeated rhyme schemes, were beginning to bore me. He explained that he wrote sonnets because he could easily memorize a pattern of fourteen lines. I pointed out a recent poem of his that I liked and that was not a sonnet, hoping by this to encourage him in a new direction. At the time, neither of us said any more.

The New Yorker seemed unable to refrain from buying my translations of Borges's poems, so in my letters I kept up a steady stream of reports and even better from Elsa's point of view a steady flow of cheques. My letters to her were a litany of pleas for books by Borges that I required. Her letters to me were a still greater litany of the make-up that she required. No matter how much I assured her there would be no problem about the cosmetics, she wrote to me on three different occasions about what to bring her, calling her requests *algunas cositas* – 'a few little things'.

She even included tiny drawings on the page so that an obvious incompetent like me – someone with one foot in Georgie's dream world – could not fail her.

Her letters were always affectionate and full of good cheer, except for when she was overcome by memories of Cambridge. Writing to me clearly triggered recollections she felt she could safely, if painfully, share. She signed in various ways: 'Elsa', 'Elsa and Georgie', 'Elsa, Georgie, and Ricardo', and 'Elsa and family'.

Of course, each time she wrote, the list of *cositas* grew. On 23 September, after telling me that two days earlier she and Georgie had celebrated their first wedding anniversary with a drinks party, she leapt in the next sentence to beg me to bring the things she asked for without fear of the expense, since she still had dollars to pay me back. (Elsa's letters were a marvel of diving in successive sentences from one topic to something entirely different. She also shared with Emily Dickinson an inability to conclude her sentences with full stops – both women were enamoured of dashes.) Elsa also had a penchant for writing letters on the printed stationery of hotels, airlines, and on one occasion of a government office. Here is the first shopping list, punctuation mostly her own:

> 1 of those little baskets with a cloth cover so that bread will not get cold. [Her accompanying drawing looked like a squash racket with stitches down the centre.]

3 or 4 bottles of perfume – *Dior* – *Lanvin* – *Intrigue* – which cost me 3 to 4 dollars each (with atomizer – if now they cost a little more it doesn't matter –) These are of great interest to me) – (If you can bring more so much the better) –

1 white plastic case with umbrella (I saw them in Touraine but they are everywhere) [This time her artwork had me baffled; her sketch looked like a handbag with an attachment on the outside you could slip an umbrella through.] It must *not* be one of those used for boots [more artwork; this time the bag was triangular] this kind *no* – For now I can't remember anything else but later I will in another letter.

And on 7 October she did. 'Another request' and then on the left of the page the artwork in a little box. The drawing consisted of two closed eyelids with prominent lashes, the one on the left marked 'Right Eve' (sic), the one on the right marked 'Left Eve' (sic). Above this were the words 'Natural Hair Lasher | Before handling read leaflet under tray'. Below, written on the outline of a tube, 'Maybelline Lash Adhesive'. As if all this were not enough, to the right of what appeared in the box, Elsa instructed, '(I bought it in *Five and Ten* of Harvard (around the corner from the Coop) – the top is of transparent plastic – *don't be afraid to spend* – I will reimburse you the minute you arrive –'

Was that going to be all? It was until 22 October, when

her obsession once more got the better of her. 'Don't forget, please, my requests,' she wrote. And she reiterated that if I wanted she could send me a dollar money order in advance or pay me the equivalent in Argentine money on my arrival. 'Do you remember what I asked for? Just to be sure I will repeat it.' And, heart-stoppingly, this 'logical' woman did just that.

This time she told me the Maybelline Lash Adhesive were false eyelashes and, 'logically', they came two to the box. She wanted two boxes (Five and Ten). As for the perfumes, Marcel Rochas and Schiaparelli were added (they were two to three ounces). Then she got quite specific. '*Femme* (Marcel Rochas), No. 5227 Net Wt. 2 oz.' The Schiaparelli was to be *Shocking*. The Lanvin, *Arpège*. The Christian Dior, *Miss Dior*. Numbers, prices, sizes of each item were included. This way, I thought, I could go crazy but I could not go wrong. The basket to keep the bread warm was repeated (with drawing); so was the plastic case for the umbrella (ditto drawing).

Now she was pushing it. She wanted me to bring her Christmas things, which would give her great joy – napkins and perfumed candles. She bribed me, adding 'anything else you can think of for our table, which we will share with you.'

Such was the costly price – and I don't mean in terms of money – that she was exacting from me.

I was trying in the midst of all this bazaar-haggling

to get a couple of important matters across to her. First, when I began to send her *New Yorker* cheques I wanted it to be clear that by law thirty per cent of the amount due Borges was being withheld in US taxes. I explained that I'd tried to no avail to see if anything could be done legally to circumvent this. Elsa seemed resigned and not unduly disturbed, but I knew that at some future date the fact of the disparity between what Borges was getting and what I was getting – although it was in fact an agreed fifty-fifty split – would stir up resentment in her against me.

There was a second thing I needed to tell her. My negotiations with American publishers were getting so snarled and complicated that I'd had to write to Georgie in English about these matters and send the letter to his friend and literary collaborator, the novelist Adolfo Bioy Casares, who would read and discuss it with Borges. What my report contained would have been way beyond Elsa's ken. I made sure that at the same time I was posting my letter to Bioy I was also informing Elsa about this. The facts did not trouble her in the least; I was sending my letter to Bioy and not to Leonor. In her reply Elsa thanked me for a cheque I had enclosed.

Still suffering in the immediate aftermath of Harvard, she sent a letter on 13 July and in her distraction wrote the year as '1928'. It was on stationery of the Hotel Crillon, Santiago, Chile. In closing, she said, 'Forgive me, Norman, but I can't even think about Cambridge – it has consumed all my store of tears and heartbreak – I never thought that in a place so white and pretty one could be so miserable – except for 4 or 5 dear friends everything was unhappy there – when you come I'll tell you about many things . . .'

In August I announced that I would be arriving in November but had not yet fixed a date. 'Olga awaits you with *empanadas*,' Elsa replied. 'Ricardo will be in charge of showing you around Buenos Aires – Georgie and I are still very, very happy . . .'

As for Borges, who dwelled in his own self-constructed labyrinth and could not be bothered to answer letters, I was lucky enough to receive one reply in the months we were apart. Dictated to Bioy, it was written in Georgie's stiff attempt at colloquial English.

> Your letters have given me much pleasure.
>
> Looking back on the many evenings we have spent together in Cambridge talking about literature, I feel sure your English rendering of my stuff will be really excellent.

Now Elsa was sending me a steady flow of poems by Georgie printed in *La Nación*. One was about Heraclitus; another about setting out his books in the new flat in Avenida Belgrano; still another the words of a soliloquy spoken by Jesus Christ. They were moving and with a wonderful freshness and energy about them. The moment they arrived they were translated and sent off to *The New*

Yorker. But I was curious to know whether these were brand-new poems or old draft pages that Borges had rescued from a bottom drawer.

'Heraclitus', Elsa informed me in her letter of 22 October – the one containing the long lists of requests – had been written two months earlier. So, without a word of demur, Borges had taken up my suggestion and was giving the sonnet a wide berth.

Elsa, for her part, could not break off her propensity for associative thinking. Mention of 'Heraclitus' led to her recollection and Georgie's of the headlong enthusiasm with which I tackled everything. She pictured me in the Cambridge flat, kneeling before the sofa and writing, surrounded by books. 'Did I remember her long evenings shut in and forlorn in her white kitchen? Do you remember my wretched loneliness? Now all that has passed like a sad dream.'

At last I could announce that I would be arriving at Ezeiza, on Pan Am flight 203, at 9.45 p.m. on 14 November. I told Elsa her detailed descriptions of the *cositas* were very clear. I was hoping she saw that there was no time to ask for anything more.

She didn't, and I was on my way. I felt as though I already had one foot in the Argentine.

12   Arrival

Mid-November morning, spring in the southern hemisphere, but in Buenos Aires the temperature was already that of high summer. Worse than the vehement, unforgiving heat was the mugginess, the suffocating humidity. Some sort of meteorological vengeance seemed afoot. Still, it was good to see the new leaves on the plane trees along the streets.

Georgie and Elsa had met my plane the night before and whisked me straight to the modest hotel she had found for me in the Avenida de Mayo. It was a walk of only four or five blocks from their flat. The hotel, called the Mundial, was old-fashioned and somewhat rundown but comfortable. I was on the fifth floor. If I ignored the lift and walked down to the street I made my way past a dilapidated mezzanine strewn with old dining furniture. My only disappointment with my room was the light, or near absence of it, at night. A tiny bare bulb hung down from the ceiling on a cord that was yards overhead. It made for perpetual twilight.

Elsa was transformed. Young and happy, with a glow

about her, she seemed to bounce with energy. Every vestige of the Cambridge gloom and sullenness had evaporated. Borges had put on four kilos but was as fragile as ever. He too brimmed over with enthusiasm and was full of plans for me.

He was also very solicitous of my immediate well-being. After a day or two he asked me if I slept a siesta in the afternoon. With the heat and the formal Buenos Aires dress code, I did not think there was an option. At this time in the city everyone wore suits and ties. It would have been social suicide not to. But to wear a suit and tie was also a form of suicide. On the streets or on crowded buses one melted and reached one's destination drenched through with sweat.

Borges was anxious to teach me the seriousness of the siesta and its fundamentals. You never took one in your clothes. You undressed for your nap, and if you wore pyjamas to bed you put on pyjamas for the siesta. All this turned out incredibly sound advice and I was to follow it to the letter.

My immediate task was to get orientated in two areas – the physical layout of the city and the spoken language. The city sprawled in the direction of the four points of the compass, and there was no telling how far to the south and west the buildings ceded to the plain, the fabled pampa. The Avenida de Mayo, once a grand boulevard created in the 1890s to connect the Casa Rosada, the dusky-pink Government House, with the Congress – a distance of some fifteen blocks – was an old mistress who had known better days.

By night, when the area around the Mundial came alive, the street became all flashy neon lights. This nook of the city, I was to find out, was riddled with Spanish immigrants. Native Argentines – in their tiresome innate superiority – looked down on and called these Spaniards *gallegos*. *Gallego* means Galician, for that was the region of Spain from which these people largely came, turning themselves into lowly shopkeepers and domestic servants. The word *gallego* is something of an offensive slur and in general is applied to denizens from Spain. Borges once told me that his fellow Argentines usually referred not to *gallegos* but to *gallegos de mierda* – lousy Spics.

The side streets around the Mundial, running north and south, were narrow and dusty and already in the early morning they teemed and throbbed with activity. Café-bars, dark and cool, were doing a brisk business in coffee and croissants – *medialunas*, or half moons, in the local lingo – and their marble counters brimmed with stacks of sandwiches under glass domes in anticipation of mid-morning trade.

I was all eyes and ears, all antennae tuned, and despite the general shabbiness and decay, the musty smell that rushed out of empty shop fronts on currents of dank air, old cement plaster crumbling away from underlying brick, a sense of endless greyness as only the concrete heart of Buenos Aires can be grey, I was filled with wonder. The language, however, baffled me – that machine-gun-fast, slangy *porteño* Spanish that I was unused to and that seemed to sail over my head as I caught three words in every ten.

Borges had warned me not to expect much. On my first morning, he led me on a tour of the city's south side, where he himself had recently moved. It was obvious as we set off from the National Library, of which he was director and where most of our work would be done, that any glory or grandeur the city had to offer lay in its past. It was in this past that Borges revelled. We made our slow way to the Parque Lezama, in the historic old part of Buenos Aires. The park precinct sprawled down a bank, faded, dessicated, dying.

It was here on a gravel path that Borges asked me what the word was for what our feet trod on. 'Gravel,' I told him. 'No,' he said, 'it's another word. Peeble?' 'Ah, you mean pebble.' 'That's it. I had only read the word and never heard it spoken.'

The city's pavements were laid in yellow-brown tiles, but everywhere they were broken or missing, uneven or loose. These same pavements were also so narrow that it was difficult to negotiate them two abreast, even when interminable stretches of them were not being excavated in an effort to patch up the municipal viscera – the sewers, water mains, electric and telephone cables. Neglect was no newcomer, it seemed, and everything struck me as old-fashioned, out of date, dingy, ill-lit, underfunded. After our walk I went home to lunch with him and Elsa.

The Borges flat, in the 1300 block of the Avenida Belgrano, was on the eighth floor, at the front – or street side – of the building. It had a small balcony that opened off the living room but this balcony, owing to the busy street traffic below, was so noisy and exposed to the soot that drifted up from the myriad of passing buses that it could seldom be used.

One of Borges's biographers characterized the flat as 'elegant'. It was not. He also implied that Borges moved there with Elsa straight after their wedding. In fact, the flat was not ready for occupancy until the couple returned from Harvard. Borges commemorated the moment in his poem 'June 1968', in which 'a man sets up his books / on the waiting shelves'. Elsa had written to me in that same month to say that she and Georgie were living out of suitcases while she set about arranging the furniture.

In addition to the living room, with a small dining area at one end, there was a kitchen and there were two bedrooms, one fronting on the street and a smaller one at the back. This is where Borges slept. He had some glass-fronted bookshelves here that housed the *Britannica* and his broken set of Burton's Thousand Nights and a Night. Among these holy of holies it was his habit to slip banknotes, the old ten-thousand peso bills, between the pages of a certain volume, hoping that this little stockpile was out of Elsa's reach.

The kitchen, near the entrance, was a small utilitarian affair like all middle-class kitchens in Buenos Aires. The custom, with ample cheap restaurants, was to eat out. On entering the flat, off to the left was the minuscule maid's room. When I came on the scene, Betty, a pleasant girl in her early twenties, occupied these quarters.

The living area was covered in a battleship-grey, wall-to-wall carpet. But the flat had no vacuum cleaner. Betty's method of cleaning the floor was to sweep the carpet with a broom. This removed dust from the carpet, while at the same time evenly redistributing it onto the bottom row of the bookshelves that lined the right-hand living-room wall.

Elsa lost little time in escorting me into her bedroom. Along one whole wall built-in cupboards had been installed. These were her pride and joy. Or was it their contents that were her pride and joy?

'Look, di Giovanni,' she demonstrated. 'This is Walt Whitman. And this is Edgar Allan Poe. And this one is Nathaniel Hawthorne.'

She was referring to coats. The clothes in this wardrobe were so tightly packed that she could barely get a finger between the distinguished figures who hung there. She knew of course that I understood what she was talking about. Every word, spoken with a thrill in her voice, was a demonstration of her cleverness. Each of these literary garments represented a fee she had collected in the United States for one of Georgie's lectures.

13　Settling In

Borges was as good as his word. In one of her letters to me Elsa had written, 'Yesterday Georgie was saying that when you come he's going to introduce you to the best Argentine writers ...'

A night or two after my arrival I was having dinner with Adolfo Bioy Casares and his wife Silvina Ocampo at their palatial but rundown top-floor flat in Calle Posadas. According to Elsa, Georgie ate there every night. I know Borges must have spoken well of me to them because they welcomed me like an old friend. I began to accompany Borges there two or three evenings a week but I don't think he ever told the Bioys beforehand that I would be along.

Dinner in Buenos Aires never took place before 8.30, so that by the time you finished it would be past midnight. At that hour we all marched down to the street floor, where Bioy kept a car in the palazzo's garage, and he would chauffeur us home, dropping me off first at the Mundial, and then swinging around to Borges's flat in Avenida Belgrano.

Bioy, a novelist and story writer, was one of the handsomest men in the city. He was also Don Juan personified. Silvina was a poet and painter. As well, she wrote quirky stories. By some arrangement of their own, she and Bioy lived quite separate lives. Borges always claimed that Bioy owned the finest library of English books in South America. It was housed in a towering set of bookshelves that covered one entire wall of the flat's antechambers. The books were arranged alphabetically by author, regardless of subject, so that Bioy's maid could find and send him any volume he asked for during his summer stays in Mar del Plata or at his estancia.

Silvina, eleven years older than Bioy, was the darling of a much younger set of writers than those Borges knew. Georgie maintained that this youthful generation were all Communists and that Silvina was attempting to ingratiate herself with them in case of a sudden revolution. Borges was not without his absurd fixations. There was something about Silvina that from time to time annoyed Borges and caused him to make scathing remarks about her. One of these angry remarks was that she and her family were Jews. He didn't much care for Silvina's stories and made fun of the scansion of her poems.

At Bioy's I was also introduced to the melancholic Manuel Peyrou, who wrote detective novels and worked at *La Prensa*. According to Borges, Peyrou had a wife with whom he did not live and yet was not estranged from. The woman had been his mistress for years, and one day he married her, while choosing still to live apart.

Carlos Mastronardi, a poet and journalist, had been a youthful pal of Borges's when they roamed the city streets on endless all-night walks during the Twenties. Mastronardi, at the time I met him, lived a nocturnal existence in the reaches of the Avenida de Mayo. He had the whey-face of a man who never saw the sun. These writer-friends of Borges's were all unfailingly kind to me and every one of them made me gifts of signed copies of their books.

Elsa had written to me that most nights she went to dinner at the Bioys' with Georgie. But this no longer held true by the time I arrived. I don't think she fell out with the Bioys; it was probably more a question of mutual boredom. Once more, in the high-powered literary discussions that took place around the Bioys' table, Elsa would have had nothing to say and though she might have tried to draw the accommodating Silvina out on domestic topics Silvina would very quickly have found such conversation less than pointless.

Borges also shepherded me around to the offices of his publishers, Emecé, where the printing presses rumbled away in the next room and where typescripts of Georgie's books went unread straight into the hands of compositors. His editor, Carlos Frías, spoke a snappy, friendly English. A likeable character, Frías was a dapper little man barely five-feet tall and had a formidable reputation as a ladykiller.

I imagine he obliged society women who were desperate to get their novels and poems published. Borges once recounted to me a heated session that took place between two such authors. One claimed that she was being published by Emecé. Yes, came back the other, so was she, but she did not have to pay to get her work printed. Frías taught English literature at one or two universities. To make ends meet, everyone in publishing – and in most else in the city – held down several jobs.

The rounds with Borges brought me to the premises of *Sur*, the once great magazine, it too now moribund and reduced to publishing quarterly. Here I was introduced to the venerable Victoria Ocampo, an older sister of Silvina, and to Enrique Pezzoni, the review's witty, handsome young editor. He as well, like Borges himself, doubled as a university lecturer. To Borges Victoria was always Queen Victoria, and he also found her annoying. He never forgot – and still chafed at the idea – that in *Sur*'s early days she would print pieces by others, especially European notables, at the front of the magazine while his work languished in the back pages.

One of the first things Borges did on the morning after my arrival was to take me into a shop where he bought me a pack of Spanish playing cards. It was a mysterious and inexplicable gesture. We certainly never used the cards and he never afterward mentioned them. I know they represented to him an old Buenos Aires that had disappeared.

The cards were colourful and exotic, but I could never figure out the suits. There were beautiful red, green, and yellow cups laid out symmetrically. There were swords, their blades blue, set out head to tail. The clubs were literally that – stubby logs from a tree, with the branches lopped and some sprouting leaves. Of what seemed equivalent to our jacks, queens, and kings, the figures were all elaborately dressed males brandishing swords or clubs. One of these figures rode horses that looked like those found on a merry-go-round. One suit totally defied me – a round symbol with serrations all round, looking like the blade of a circular saw. Unstated, sentimentally, I think Borges was attempting to introduce me into his world. He once wrote that long ago, before the advent of magazines, the gauchos used a playing card as a picture, which they nailed to a wall in their shacks.

Another thing Borges did early on was to introduce me to an old-time Argentine dessert called *queso y dulce*, commonly known as *postre de vigilante*. These were stiff slabs of jam, *membrillo* (quince) and *batata* (sweet potato), laid atop a slab of any of several firm cheeses, such as Mar del Plata or Edam. He explained that they were called *postres de vigilante* – policeman's desserts – because a night watchman could conveniently make his rounds carrying these goodies wrapped in paper in one of his pockets. In no time I had a taste for both of them.

Evenings at least once a week I was invited by Borges to

book launches, where the atmosphere was informal and a small circle of friends stood around speaking out in turns as the spirit moved them in praise of the book or author we were there to honour. There was a warmth about these gatherings, a few like-minded men and women at the far ends of the earth carrying their grain of sand to the altar of literature, of civilization. Elsa of course was never to be seen at these venues.

You never knew where Borges was going to lead. One evening soon after my arrival he dragged me along to a television channel to attend the grand finale of a popular quiz programme sponsored by the toothpaste company Odol. The obligatory screaming audience and a young man answering questions about Borges's short stories. Of course, to spice up the proceedings, the announcer stuck a microphone in my face and asked if I were a professor at Harvard. Borges quickly cut in to whisper in my ear, 'Avoid veracity.' I responded in the affirmative and so for five glorious minutes I became a Harvard man. The boy who won later joined Borges's informal class in Old Norse. He was sixteen and an insufferable prig.

Finding my way around alone, especially at night, seemed insuperable. So did *porteño*-speak. The language Borges spoke to me, and the vocabulary I came upon in his writing, was not the current lingo of either people on the street or the younger writers I was beginning to meet. Sometimes when I was conversing, my interlocutor would ask, 'Where on earth did you get that word? Only you and Borges and his mother would know what it means.'

As for topographic progress, I often found myself on an unknown street corner after dark, unsure which way my hotel lay. To complicate matters, north and south of long, narrow Avenida Rivadavia, which bisected the city, the same thoroughfare changed its name. To the north, farther from the centre, where the streets bent to meet the curve of the broad River Plate, I invariably went adrift. The layout of Buenos Aires, a series of chessboard patterns that did not match one another, the sheer size and sprawl of the city, coupled with a certain sameness and an absence of natural landmarks, kept me long confused.

As for Elsa's friendly promise that her son would act as my cicerone, it never happened. One night, at loose ends, I strolled a number of blocks along Talcahuano to what had once been the Hotel California. Elsa had lived here in a bed-sit before marrying Georgie, and now Ricardo was in residence. I found him at home. We went out on the street to a bar and had a drink together. I could see his mind was on something else, something faraway. I imagined it was some woman. We did not seem to have much to say to each other so did not tarry long. After that encounter I never set eyes on Ricardo again.

14   The Recoleta

On one of the very first mornings after my arrival in Buenos Aires Borges eagerly took me on a tour of the Recoleta Cemetery.

The burial ground, on the former northern outskirts of Buenos Aires, had once been the site of the garden of the Iglesia de Nuestra Señora del Pilar, a church built by monks of the Order of the Augustinian Recollects between 1722 and 1732. The cemetery today, set in fourteen acres, has more than 4,600 burial vaults. The elaborate tombs set above ground cheek by jowl in marble and granite, in a variety of architectural styles, form a true city of the dead, and its inhabitants make up a veritable history of Argentina.

We made our way through the neoclassical entrance, with its Doric columns, passing under the motto *Expectamus Dominum* – We Await the Lord. It was a pleasant morning, with chirping birds and not too hot in the shade of the Recoleta's trees. Cats lolled on every hand, more plentiful than in the cellars of the National Library. On first sight the cemetery seems a labyrinth of paths and passageways and little diagonal avenues. But we immediately turned left and Borges led me directly to his family crypt.

On a marble lintel over the doorway were the words 'Tomb of D[on] Isidoro Suárez and Family'. Clustered like limpets on the façade was a series of commemorative bronze plaques, for several of Borges's ancestors were founding fathers and military heroes. It was with a subdued, quiet pride that Borges ushered me to the tomb. What he was doing, in reality, was introducing me to his family, to his past, to his Argentine past.

One of his best early poems, dating from the beginning of the 1920s and included in his first published book, *Fervor de Buenos Aires* (1923), celebrated this cemetery:

Convinced of our mortality
by so many confirmations of final dust,
we drop our voices, our steps grow slow
between the slow rows of family crypts,
whose rhetoric of shadow and stone
promises or prefigures the coveted
dignity of being dead.

And poignantly it ended with these lines:

These thoughts came to me in the Recoleta,
in the place where my ashes will lie.

Borges also celebrated the life and deeds of his Recoleta ancestors in many of his poems, some of which are among his finest work.

Foremost amongst these ancestors perhaps is his maternal great-grandfather, Isidoro Suárez, who was born in Buenos Aires in 1799, an exact century before Borges. Suárez's army career began in 1814 as a cadet in the Horse Grenadiers, and by 1816 he was in Mendoza as part of the Army of the Andes, which was preparing to cross the cordillera to liberate Chile from Spanish domination. In the Chilean campaign, Suárez fought at Chacabuco (February 1817) and a few days later led a daring exploit, the capture in Valparaiso harbour of a Spanish brigantine of war, in which his force of fourteen soldiers and seven sailors overcame the ship's crew of eighty-nine. This won him advancement to second lieutenant.

In 1818 he took part in the defeat of Cancha Rayada (March) and the victory of Maipú (April), acting with such gallantry in the latter battle that he was immediately promoted to first lieutenant. The next year he fought at Bío-Bío and at Chillán, and, in 1820, embarked on the Peruvian campaign, where, in December, he fought at Pasco – again with distinction – and was made captain. During the following two years he took part in at least six other actions, and again moved up in rank. In 1824 under Bolívar's command, Suárez became the hero of the day in the famous battle of Junín; he later fought at Ayacucho, and by the year's end had been promoted by Bolívar to colonel.

The War of Independence now over, Suárez remained in Peru another two years, until, accused of having been part of a conspiracy against Bolívar, he was exiled to Chile, from which he returned to Buenos Aires in 1827. There he was received with distinction, and, crossing over into Uruguay, he fought in the war against the Brazilian empire.

At this time Suárez also became active in the Unitarian cause; in 1829 he fought at Las Palmitas, in the Province of Buenos Aires, where he defeated a minor Federalist caudillo. This was a period of great upheaval and chaos in Argentine history, when the two factions – the Federalists and the Unitarians – were locked in a long, complicated, bitter civil war. The Unitarians favoured a strong centralist government, with liberal institutions and free trade. Their adherents included a large part of the wealthy and cultured families of Buenos Aires. Federalist policy, appealing to conservative, traditionalist values, had as its economic basis the more primitive one of cattle production for the export of hides and salt meat. The leader of the Federalists was the powerful caudillo Juan Manuel de Rosas. In 1835 Rosas instituted a seventeen-year reign of terror, during which he ruled the country with an iron hand.

When the Unitarians lost power Suárez emigrated to Uruguay. In 1834, marrying into an old Uruguayan family, he settled on the land. He still continued to take part in the resistance against Rosas into the 1840s, but in ill health he retired to Montevideo, where he died in 1846. Suárez had been decorated more than twenty times. His remains were brought back to Argentina in 1879, and a town was named for him in the south of the Province of Buenos Aires. His brother Manuel, a sergeant major and also a Unitarian, was executed by Rosas in 1842.

The battle of Junín was fought in the highlands of Peru on 6 August 1824. The Royalist forces were made up of two cavalry units, totalling 1,300 men; the Republicans, of a number of cavalry squadrons, numbering 900 men, under General Necochea. Two of these squadrons, the Hussars of Peru, were held in reserve back of a marshy stretch of land at the southern end of the battlefield. These reserve forces were commanded by the young Suárez. The Republicans were bottled up in a narrow pass between a hill on one side and a marsh cut by a stream on the other, and were thus unable to get out onto the open plain. It was five o'clock in the afternoon. Only two squadrons were able to meet the onrushing Royalists, and both of them were driven back. At this point, the second Republican general, Miller, began his attack; but his forces were also broken up. In the midst of this disorder and confusion, Necochea's trumpets sounded the call to reform, but his efforts were smashed by the Royalists, into whose hands he fell prisoner with a number of sabre wounds. The air rang with the dry sound of steel against steel and the anger and cursing of men.

Now from the marshes came Suárez's Hussars, attacking the Royalists from behind, cutting the enemy down with sabres and lances, and breaking their force. Encouraged by the spectacle, the rest of the Republican cavalry regrouped and from the front and flanks charged the regiments that Suárez was dispersing. Necochea was rescued; the battle lasted only forty-five minutes. The Royalist losses were nineteen officers and 345 soldiers killed, and eighty taken prisoner; the Republicans lost three officers and forty-two soldiers, while eight officers and ninety-one soldiers were wounded. Bolívar commended Suárez, saying that 'when history describes the glorious battle of Junín . . . it will be attributed to the bravery and audacity of this young officer; as of today, you will no longer be the Hussars of Peru but will be called the Lancers of Junín'.

Borges made use of the rich experience of his great-grandfather's life in at least two stories and in his 1953 poem, 'A Page to Commemorate Colonel Suárez, Victor at Junín'.

Borges's paternal grandfather, Francisco Borges, was another of his distinguished forebears. He was born in Montevideo in 1833 and became an artillery cadet in 1850 during Oribe's siege of the city. Two years later, Borges fought with an Uruguayan division at Caseros, when Rosas was overthrown. In 1855, moving to the Argentine, he offered 'his arm and his sword to the government of the State of Buenos Aires'. In 1857 he found himself a second lieutenant in the army of Colonel (later General) Emilio Mitre, and under Mitre's command he fought against the cacique Coliqueo in the battle of the Cañada de los Leones and, the next year, in a further expedition against the Indians.

From this point on, Borges took part in all the important battles (including Cepeda and Pavón) and many of the lesser engagements of the internecine civil wars between Buenos Aires province and the Argentine confederation, becoming a captain in 1861 and sergeant major in 1863. In 1865 he fought in the war with Paraguay at Corrientes (25 May), Yatay (17 August), and Uruguayana (18 September); the next year, at Paso de la Patria and Itapirú (16-17 April), Estero Bellaco (2 May), Tuyutí (24 May), and Boquerón (16-18 July). He was wounded in each of these last two battles, the second time severely enough to force him into a long convalescence back in Buenos Aires, where he was promoted to lieutenant colonel. From February 1867 to the end of the year, he was back at the front; in 1868 he was made colonel. The next year he was given command of the southern frontier of Buenos Aires, and in June 1870 he was sent to relieve caudillo López Jordán's siege of Paraná. There he met an Englishwoman, Frances (Fanny) Haslam, whom he married the next year. In this same year, 1871, Borges was made commander in chief of the northern and western frontiers of Buenos Aires and the southern frontier of Santa Fe, fighting in punitive expeditions against cattle-raiding Indians. In this capacity, he fought the important battle of San Carlos, 8 March 1872. The next year, Borges was back in Entre Ríos, putting down another rebellion by López Jordán, but by early 1874 he was able to return to his frontier outpost.

To this point, Borges was the professional soldier – 'an object dragged from battle to battle', as described in one of his grandson's poems. Then, in the last year of his life, he became involved in a revolt against the government that was to force him into suicide. The 1874 elections became a test between Domingo Sarmiento, who, as president, could not succeed himself, and General Bartolomé Mitre (Emilio's brother), who had been president before Sarmiento and who announced his new candidacy. Sarmiento, in control of patronage and the election machinery, was backing Nicolás Avellaneda, who was ultimately elected and inaugurated in October 1874. Meanwhile, Mitre had enlisted Borges's support for his revolution, which was to take place on 12 October, expecting Borges to bring with him the troops at his command. When the government discovered the plot, Colonel Borges was summoned and asked what attitude he would assume in the conflict. 'Until October 12,' he said, 'the government may count on my loyalty and on the troops entrusted to my honour.' But events precipitated the revolt, and Borges, since he had given Sarmiento his word, found he could not fulfil his promises to his personal and political friends. Instead, he handed over his troops to the government and resigned his command. Misunderstanding his action, his friends branded him a traitor.

On 12 October, alone, Borges joined the uprising, putting himself as a private citizen under General Mitre's orders. The next month he was in command of a brigade, under Mitre, at the battle of La Verde (26 November 1874). Towards the close of that day, Mitre ordered a retreat; Borges pointed out that the enemy was about to run out of fire power, but his judgement went unheeded. It was at this point, when the general repeated his order, that Borges mounted his horse and, accompanied by several of his loyal soldiers, slowly rode out, arms across his chest, towards the enemy lines. The revolt failed. Mitre was imprisoned for several months, but his life was spared. Borges died from his wounds two days later. In his last words, he said, 'I have fallen in the belief of having fulfilled my duty and my convictions, and for the same principles that I have fought all my life.'

Another of Borges's illustrious forebears, to whom he was related through his maternal grandfather, was Francisco Narciso de Laprida, the subject of Borges's accomplished 'Conjectural Poem', published in 1943.

Laprida was born in 1786 in the western Argentine province of San Juan, studied in Chile, and received his law degree there in 1810. Returning to the city of San Juan the next year, he practised his profession and in 1812 he was elected municipal magistrate (*alcalde*). In the following years, he assisted in the support of José de San Martín's Army of the Andes, which was preparing to liberate Chile, and he was elected member and then president of the congress that met in Tucumán, in 1816, and declared the independence of the 'United Provinces of South America'. In 1824 he was representative of the Province of San Juan in the constituent assembly, meeting in Buenos Aires, of which he was made president. He was a signer of the 1826 constitution, but the next year, upon failure of the Unitarian cause (the constitution proved too centralist in spirit for the ruling caudillos), Laprida retired to San Juan. Under threat of persecution by Facundo Quiroga, the ruthless caudillo who ruled an eight-province region of the Andes, Laprida was eventually forced to flee to Mendoza, where he headed a small division in defence of the invasion by Quiroga. In 1829 Laprida found himself dug in against other Federalist forces; trying to escape after an attack in violation of an armistice, Laprida was hunted down and killed by a troop of gauchos. His body was never found.

Borges's poem commemorating Laprida is in the form of a dramatic monologue. Here are some of its closing lines:

I who longed to be someone else, to weigh
judgements, to read books, to hand down the law,
will lie in the open out in these swamps;
but a secret joy somehow swells my breast.

I see at last that I am face to face
with my South American destiny.
I was carried to this ruinous hour
by the intricate labyrinth of steps
woven by my days from a day that goes
back to my birth. At last I've discovered
the mysterious key to all my years,
the fate of Francisco de Laprida,
the missing letter, the perfect pattern
that was known to God from the beginning.
In this night's mirror I can comprehend
my unsuspected true face. The circle's
about to close. I wait to let it come.

Isidoro Acevedo (1828-1905), Borges's maternal grand-father, was another of his ancestors who earned literary immortality in his grandson's poetry. Of him, Borges has recorded:

One day, at the age of nine or ten, he walked by the Plata Market. It was in the time of Rosas. Two gaucho teamsters were hawking peaches. Young Isidoro lifted the canvas covering the fruit, and there were the decapitated heads of Unitarians, with blood-stained beards and wide-open eyes. The boy ran home, climbed up into the grapevine growing in the back patio, and it was only later that night that he could bring himself to tell what he had seen in the morning. In time, he was to see many things during the civil wars, but none ever left so deep an impression on him.

Another impressive burial spot in the Recoleta is that of the Federalist General Facundo Quiroga, who is said to be interred in a standing position. When Domingo Faustino Sarmiento published his famous book *Civilization or Barbarism* in 1845, it was Juan Facundo Quiroga whom he had chosen as the central figure in the history and the man who best represented the ruthless figure of the cuadillo.

Facundo Quiroga (1793-1835), known as the 'Tiger of the Plains', was born in La Rioja, and during the 1820s had extended his power over a large region of the Andes. So cruel was his reputation (he typically ordered the throats cut of all prisoners who fell into his hands), so awesome was his presence, that he bred fear wherever he went. Although nominally a Federalist, Quiroga became a threat and an annoyance to Rosas, and, in 1835, on his return to Córdoba from a meeting with Rosas in Buenos Aires, Quiroga was ambushed and murdered by the local ruling gang, the Reinafé brothers. Though Rosas was quick to order a costly funeral for the fallen general and to demand the death sentence for the assassins, it had always been believed that it was he who had arranged for Quiroga's death. Years later, from exile in Southampton, Rosas wrote, 'They say I ordered the assassination of the illustrious General Quiroga. But have they proved it?'

Borges was intrigued by Quiroga, fascinated by what he represented in the blood-soaked history of the Argentine. He wrote two poems about him, and here are some lines of the unreprinted earlier composition, first published in *Luna de enfrente* (1925):

> Over these plains Juan Facundo Quiroga unleashed an empire
>   made of lances.
> An outlaw empire, a poverty-ridden empire.
> An empire whose living drums were the hoofbeats of mustangs
>   beating a ruffle round humbled cities . . .
> An empire of the knife that feasts on waiting, trembling throats . . .

For a while, upon his heady return from several years in Europe, Borges went through a nationalistic phase that, much to his credit, he eventually outgrew. He had embraced all things Argentine, good and bad, but eventually recognized his error. In Argentina super-nationalists are constantly baying for a strong man to lead them. This is a code word meaning a dictator. When Rosas' remains were repatriated in 1989 from his grave in Southampton (he died there in 1877), Argentine nationalist-patriots rejoiced. These remains are now in the Recoleta.

It is easy to see, with Borges's legacy of his ancestors' exploits, in what direction he might have turned. He did have his confused moments. Once at the University of Georgetown, in Washington, where we were giving a poetry reading, Borges flew into anger at the remarks 'made against my country' by one of the speakers, a professor at the University of Tucumán, which the military government had closed down. I had to point out to Borges what the professor was railing against, and that the Argentine also happened to be this man's country. On the other hand, Borges remarked to me on several occasions about his military forebears that he and they probably would not have had much to say to each other.

There was another occasion when Borges asked me to skip our work session at the Library because he was expecting a visit from an army colonel. The man had been insulted by someone and wanted Borges to help him pen a letter challenging the man to a duel. Borges was much amused by the officer's presumptions. When we met to work the next day Borges told me the colonel had written in his letter that he would meet his adversary anywhere the man chose – 'in Buenos Aires or in any other country'.

To end this stroll in the Recoleta I would like to mention Elvira de Alvear. She was a wealthy Argentine society woman, born in 1907 and who died in 1959. Elvira was a minor poet who lived for years in Paris, where she knew Valery Larbaud, James Joyce, and Alfonso Reyes. She and Borges were friends for a long period and in 1934 he wrote a foreword to a volume of her poetry. Borges dedicated a moving poem to her in his 1960 collection *El hacedor*. It is reproduced on a bronze plaque on a wall

of the Alvear family tomb in the Recoleta. Elvira died mad,
scribbling undecipherable gibberish into a notebook. The
poem opens:

> She once had everything but one by one
> each thing abandoned her. We saw her armed
> with beauty. The morning and the hard light
> of noon from their pinnacle revealed to her
> the glorious kingdoms of the world. Evening
> wiped them away . . .
> Each thing deserted her except for one.
> A warmhearted grace was at her side
> until her final days, beyond her madness
> and decline, in an almost angelic way.
> Of Elvira what I saw first, years and years
> past, was her smile and it is now the last.

15   Cracks in the Façade

On the work front Borges was abundantly busy. I had come to Buenos Aires with a list of nearly twenty poems of his that were unpublished in book form. With some prodding I convinced him he should write another fifteen or so and bring out a new volume. He hadn't published a book under his name alone for nine years. He was unsure of these recent poems, but all the friends round Bioy's table thought my idea a good one. As did Carlos Frías.

Borges and I had been working together at the Biblioteca Nacional both mornings and late afternoons on our translations of his work into English. We juggled between the new poems, a handful of essays, and some short stories that had never before appeared in English. I now put it to him that he must spend the mornings dictating new poems to his secretaries, while I would restrict myself to seeing him only later in the day.

Enticed by his recent poetry, and buoyed up by the excitement of Buenos Aires, I had allowed the volume of selected poems to drift a bit. Meanwhile, we were under contract – and pressure – to translate his *Book of Imaginary Beings*. We began work on it late in February 1969. I devoted my mornings at the Mundial to researching and writing drafts of the book's more than one hundred short pieces, which he and I spent the afternoons revising and rewriting in English. Borges was also dashing away from time to time to deliver lectures. The word busy was a feeble understatement. With the *Imaginary Beings* alone we were running a marathon and we did not finish the book until late May.

Elsa had given me permission to receive my post at the Belgrano address, where I collected it each afternoon when I fetched Borges for our long walk to the Library. One day a copy of *The New York Review of Books* arrived. It contained a translation of 'Elvira de Alvear', a poem about Georgie's old friend of years and years before. Borges told me he preferred not to have that copy of the *NYR* at home because 'Elsa will just hide it away and besides she won't fancy a poem about another woman.'

The very next day he reported Elsa's anger at having to look for a misplaced manuscript by Susana Bombal. Susana Bombal was yet another of Borges's stable of old-time society women who from time to time summoned him to afternoon tea. 'Even if it were here,' Elsa seethed, 'do you expect me to look for the manuscript of a person who has insulted me?'

Susana Bombal lived in Buenos Aires but owned a stylish estancia in the far western Province of Mendoza.

Whenever one of her invitations came, Borges would dash from the Library at breakneck speed to hail a taxi. A day later he would relish describing to me their meeting, during which she'd read him one of her stories. After a paragraph or so, according to his account, she would pause to explain what she had written. Then she would read a page and again explain, read another and explain. Had it not been for the explanations, Borges recounted with a laugh, he would have understood nothing.

Susana, who had an Indian's dark, weathered skin, also had a chiselled masculine-looking face. In one of her rages, Elsa had cleverly referred to her as that *indio muerto*. The words need explaining in English. Elsa had deliberately used the masculine form of the noun, thereby dubbing Susana 'a dead male Indian'.

As for Elsa's jealousy of other women, one afternoon while waiting for Borges to appear after his nap I was perusing his living-room bookshelves. I spotted a copy of his most famous collection of essays in its pristine red paper cover. When I opened the book I noticed that the dedication page was missing. The volume, which dated back to 1952, had been dedicated to Margot Guerrero, who had also co-authored with Borges the Spanish original of *The Book of Imaginary Beings*. 'Ah,' Borges explained, 'Elsa tore the page out in a fit of rage.'

I noticed at some point that the letters from *The New Yorker* that I was receiving at Borges's were being carefully opened and then resealed with a strip of Sellotape. 'This military government,' Elsa told me in a tone of disgust. 'Censorship.' I also noticed that when I got my own flat in the middle of May and was receiving my post there the military government no longer seemed to show any interest in my *New Yorker* letters. It had been nosy Elsa wanting to investigate what cheques I was getting.

Margot Guerrero, who was far from well off, would once in a while stop in at the National Library to collect her royalties from Borges for her collaboration with him on *The Book of Imaginary Beings*. One day Elsa cornered me in the flat and turned on the inquisition.

'Did anyone come to the Library to see Georgie yesterday? A woman? Who was it?'

I mumbled my ignorance.

'I know he saw someone at the Library and paid her some money,' Elsa went on.

I had barely finished wondering how she knew when she led me to the door of Borges's room. It was ajar.

'When Georgie comes home,' she said, 'he sometimes puts peso notes between the pages of one of those books of his. After he leaves, I go in and count what he has secreted away. Later I recount it. Yesterday twenty-five thousand pesos were missing. Who came to the Library yesterday and to whom did he give money?'

She knew of course it had been Margot Guerrero but I refused to be drawn. Then to prove to me she was no fool,

Elsa went on to say that every time Borges telephoned his mother from the extension in his bedroom she went to her room and lifted her own receiver. She had made it a habit to eavesdrop on every word Leonor and Georgie spoke.

By this time I knew very well what Elsa and Leonor thought of each other. The mother had had her informant in Cambridge, who'd reported to her everything that had taken place there. To me, privately, doña Leonor always referred to her daughter-in-law as *ese monstruo* – 'that monster'. When I queried her why her son had married Elsa, she said, 'I didn't want him to, but he was beside himself to do so.' I'd once put the same question to Borges. 'My mother made me,' he answered.

Things were getting tense again. I asked Borges when he spoke to his mother if Elsa could hear what he was saying. Oh, no, he naively assured me, he spoke from the phone in his room. Are you absolutely certain? I pressed. I was trying to send him a message but he did not get it. I refused to come straight out and tell him what Elsa had confessed to me about monitoring his money and listening in on his conversations; I didn't want to stir up trouble.

The secretaries at the Library told me that Elsa was constantly phoning them and pressing for information. Who called on Borges today? How long had they stayed? The girls were completely loyal to Borges and kept their lips sealed, but these interventions of Elsa's upset them. They too breathed nothing of this to Borges.

That same southern hemisphere winter Elsa had a facelift. While her scars were healing, with bits of plaster holding the tucks together along her hair- and jaw-line, she cheerfully described to me the pain she was putting herself through. I was reminded of her proud moments in Cambridge when she had indulged in too many sweet-breads. Now she could barely move her lips, but she was convinced the results were going to be worthwhile. Were they? My first impression was that the finished job left her skin like parchment that had been stretched tight. Borges never said a word about any of it.

I was married shortly after to an American girl, Heather Booth. Elsa and Georgie were our witnesses. Coming out of the registry office, someone took photographs of our little group. The bride and groom and smiling witnesses made up the front row. Behind were Cousin Olga, Elsa's sister Alicia, and Teddy Paz. Teddy was a brilliant member of the younger literati. We'd met at Bioy's, and he was rapidly introducing me to a host of new writers. Elsa was wearing her precious coat of nutria fur, which did not quite come down to her knees. Georgie gripped the bride's sleeve.

A few months before, in May, Borges had written a new short story. He had given up writing stories so many years earlier that this departure became a cataclysmic event in his life. Until he realized its significance, he indulged in his inevitable bout of self-doubt; meanwhile I translated the story and sent it to *The New Yorker*. Within weeks they accepted it, and the news had a dramatic effect on Borges. Nothing could have done more at that moment to send his confidence soaring.

Then, in mid-July, I read page proofs to him of his new volume, *Elogio de la sombra*. I corrected fresh proofs towards the end of the month, and the poems were published to great acclaim in August, on Borges's seventieth birthday. Three days earlier Emecé gave the book an extravagant send-off on a stage in the Galería Van Riel, where one Dr E. Molina Mascías (whoever he was) spoke at some length and the *primera actriz* (whatever that means) María Rosa Gallo and the *primeros actores* (ditto) Enrique Fava and Luis Medina Castro read a large number of the poems. The place was packed out and a bit of a circus. On the copy of the book Borges had given me the day before, he had written '*Al colaborador*, *al amigo*, *al* promesso sposo', the last bit a reference to the fact that I was about to be married.

For Georgie's birthday, Elsa threw a little party at home with a cake iced in blue and white in the shape and colours of the book itself. On this pastry volume you could even read the title. This was not at all Borges's style, but he was nonetheless radiant. As for Elsa, she too was radiant. The facelift had paid off after all. She looked years younger and was quite stylish. Bursting with excitement and generosity, overflowing with the kindness and warmth she could be capable of, the next day she threw another party – this time for the newlyweds. She provided a wedding cake and assiduously looked after the guests, among whom were Silvina Ocampo and the novelist Manuel Puig. When someone tried to snap a picture of Silvina she extended a hand before her face, an idiosyncratic method she used to avoid being photographed.

On the living-room wall above the sofa hung a framed portrait of Elsa – just her head, with a generous mop of hair. The head was outsized. The picture may have been a pastel drawing. It had been made for Elsa by a sycophantic painter who was using her to get close to Borges, but Borges wasn't buying it.

'Larger than life,' he sneered. According to Georgie the artist would occasionally burst in on them, gaze at Elsa behind a frame he made of his thumbs and forefingers, and gush, 'Oh, Elsa, if only Velázquez could see you now!'

A few days before the wedding, Borges's sister Norah had invited me round to her studio to choose one of her paintings as a gift. Norah had a high-pitched voice that was close to a screech, but it would have been hard to find a lovelier, kinder person. When I'd arrived on the scene and she first met me, she clasped her hands before her and like an innocent child announced that the angels had sent me to look after Georgie. Norah's husband, Guillermo de Torre, who was quite deaf, had been a university professor, a widely published critic, and an early promoter of Ultraism, an avant-garde movement of the 1920s that Borges had embraced and later repudiated. Borges intensely disliked

Guillermo, first because he was a Spaniard, second because he considered him pompous, and third because Borges resented any reminder of his Ultraist period. Once, when asked how he got along with his brother-in-law, Borges famously quipped, 'We get on fine. He can't hear me and I can't see him.'

In the days that followed it was business as usual. Borges was now firmly launched on writing stories that were appearing – to everyone's delight – in the Buenos Aires press and in New York. Once more, hand in hand, came a rush of work and a whirlwind of social commitments. One of these was a flight to Casilda, a country town in the neighbouring Province of Santa Fe, where Georgie planted a eucalyptus tree in the town square. There followed an elaborate lunch, attended by a host of Casilda's dignitaries, and in the evening the honoured guest gave a lecture on the nineteenth-century poet Estanislao del Campo.

Soon our eyes began to look forward to a welcome break farther afield. That spring – it would be autumn in America – we'd all been invited to the University of Oklahoma.

16   Oklahoma and the Fur Coat

The road to Norman, Oklahoma, was long, and the negotiations – with a four-sided correspondence – protracted. A professor from the University had contacted Borges in Buenos Aires and, according to what another Oklahoma professor soon after wrote to me, 'at that time Mr Borges expressed a definite interest in a visit to our campus.' Of course he would. It was typical of Borges, who was averse to disappointing anyone, to agree to such a journey, which he really had no intention whatsoever of making.

Meanwhile, Galen Williams of the Poetry Center in New York got wind of this trip and began writing to Oklahoma to suggest I be invited with Borges. She wanted another reading from us and if she could combine forces with Oklahoma she might just pull it off. It was all a question of air fares, fees, and so forth – not to mention a willingness on Borges's part. Galen, a master of persuasion, laid it on thick. 'Borges is a dear man,' she told the Oklahoma people, 'but he doesn't want to be bothered with arrangements and more administrative things. He doesn't get cross about them, he just sort of ignores them, and then things fall apart at the last minute because Borges isn't quite sure of the date or what he is going to do . . .'

I next heard from Ivar Ivask, to whom Galen had written. He taught at the University and was also editor of the review *Books Abroad*. He had previously staged a highly successful Jorge Guillén symposium and – lightning does strike twice – had learned of me from Guillén. In his letter Ivask invited me to become part of the show.

I could not answer Galen or Ivask straightaway. Between Georgie and Elsa there were crises and complications afoot of which I was not fully aware. I had to bide my time, treading on eggshells. Borges declared himself deadly set against leaving Buenos Aires, even briefly. He had recently cancelled a trip to South Africa, refused another to Paris, and was about to notify Oxford University that he could not attend their investiture, in which he would receive an honorary degree. These cancellations were all reactions to his silent suffering with Elsa on the home front.

At last I mentioned to Borges that I'd had a letter from the University of Oklahoma.

'Yes,' said Borges, 'do me a favour, will you, di Giovanni; get me out of going there in the fall.'

'No,' said I, 'they want me to go too.'

'Oh, well then,' said Borges, 'in that case we'll have a good time.'

Borges as I first knew him at the Concord Avenue flat in Cambridge. The inscription reads: 'To N.T. di G., in friendship now and to come. J.L.B. 1967'.

With the poet Mark Strand on the stage of the YM-YWHA, New York, April 1968. Strand was a great admirer of Borges. I introduced them one morning in Borges's New York hotel room, with Borges still in his BVDs. Years earlier, Strand and I had been at university together.

The Avenida de Mayo was always a pleasant bustling place, even if it was looked down on by those who lived in the fashionable Barrio Norte. My hotel, the Mundial, was at the corner of the Avenida and Santiago del Estero, conveniently close to Borges's flat. I lived at the Mundial for about six months, where I spent my mornings translating *The Book of Imaginary Beings* and a variety of poems before going over the texts with Borges at the National Library in the late afternoons.

The Recoleta. Here lie Argentina's past and Borges's past. He was quite attached to the place, proud even, and brought the BBC here in 1979, when we spent a week in Buenos Aires recording a Radio 3 programme on the eve of his eightieth birthday. But towards the very end of his life Borges became ambivalent about Argentina and reverted to a youthful attachment to Geneva.

The Argentine National Library became a second work place for me and was a building I grew quite fond of. Borges's office opened onto the left-hand balcony. His role as director was really a sinecure; José Edmundo Clemente, as Assistant Director, ran the place and kept Borges free of official duties and concerns.

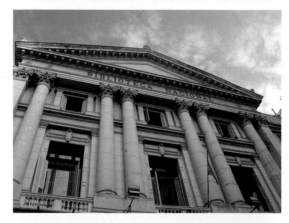

Borges at work with me at the massive conference table in his office at the National Library, 1970. It was here that Borges dictated to secretaries the poems of *Elogio de la sombra* and the stories that made up *El informe de Brodie*; it was also here that he and I spent our afternoons working on his translations into English.

My wedding day. The bride and groom flanked by Elsa and Georgie, who were the occasion's official witnesses. Behind are Cousin Olga, Elsa's sister Alicia Ibarra, and my young literary friend Teddy Paz. August 1969.

Wedding guests at the Borges's Avenida Belgrano flat. Alicia Ibarra and Cousin Olga, with her trademark cigarette and dark glasses. August 1969.

Elsa sporting her new face lift at the Belgrano flat. Cousin Olga in the background. August 1969.

A glum Elsa eating some turkey, Thanksgiving Day 1969, at the University of Oklahoma. Nick Mills, a junior lecturer, carving. When Elsa wore dark glasses indoors it was a sure sign of trouble brewing.

The same day, a rare glimpse of Borges clowning. Heather di G., cheerfully oblivious of Elsa's moods, in the background. Borges's cheer had a way of inciting Elsa to gloom.

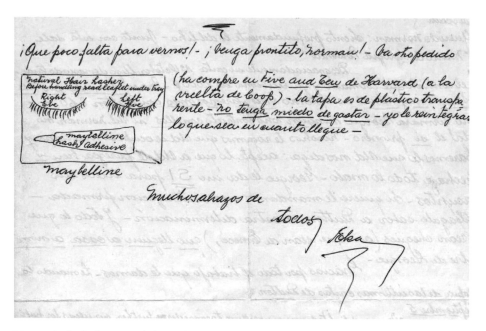

Having little faith in my ability to buy her the right cosmetics, Elsa resorted to artistry. This way I could not fail her – and to her delight I didn't. 1968.

1. Hace tres años que no puedo entrar en mi casa sin el temor de recriminaciones, de silencios hostiles y de todas ~~form~~ las formas del malhumor. Mi mujer me exige la explicación y justificación de cada una de mis palabras o/ de mis actos.

2. Es hostil a mi familia y a casi todos ~~dx~~ mis amigos; temo no recibir a muchos de ellos para evitar escenas desagradables.

3. Se inmiscuye en todos mis asuntos particulares; y ~~x~~ ha ⁀tentado que las secretarias de la Biblioteca Nacional espíen mi correspondencia, mis llamadas telefónicas y mis visitas.
  varias veces
4. Habló ᶺ con José Edmundo Clemente, el vice director de la Biblioteca Nacional, para intervenir personalmente en la dirección de esta casa.

5. Entorpeció y trató de anular mis relaciones con Norman Thomas di Giovanni, con quien estoy colaborando en la traducción de once de mis obras para la editorial Dutton de New York.

6. No ha mostrado el/menor interés ~~dn~~ en mi obra literaria, pero sí en los resultados pecuniarios de esa obra.

Borges struggled at first to produce a list of marital grievances. We hid in the National Library one Saturday morning, me at the typewriter prompting him. Finally getting the picture, he took over, and the list grew and grew and grew. 1970.

Before the monument to Borges's great-grandfather Coronel Isidoro Suárez in the sleepy prairie town named after him far to the south of Buenos Aires province. In front of the plinth, Heather di G,. Hugo Santiago, and Borges. I am second from the right. The others are the proud and generous burghers of the town and of Coronel Pringles. 1970.

Fani and myself in Borges's Maipú flat. Epifanía Úveda de Robledo was Borges and doña Leonor's loyal servant for decades. She was also a crafty character who eavesdropped on all that took place at the flat. Alas, she was surprisingly cut out of Borges's will when in the last months of his life he absented himself to Geneva, where he died.

I am overlooking Borges at a London hotel in a mood-capturing photograph taken by my friend Pamela Griffiths sometime in the 1980s. This is a characteristic pose of Borges, one hand over the other at the top of his ubiquitous walking stick.

Borges and myself rapt in attention. I see concentration in his face and contentment in mine.

'I also heard from the Poetry Center,' I told him.

'Well, you'll have to get me out of that one,' he said.

I managed to dissuade him. But when I told Elsa I too had been invited to Oklahoma, the look on her face turned sour and I could see difficulties looming ahead – perhaps the same realm of difficulties that had been worrying Georgie.

Oklahoma was proposing a stay of three weeks. In the first two Borges would deliver half a dozen lectures, three each week. He hit on 'The Literature of Argentina' as a general title for these talks, and they would consist of the following: 'The Argentine Republic', 'Gauchesco Literature', 'Sarmiento and Hernández', 'Leopoldo Lugones', 'Macedonio Fernández', and a concluding talk on himself. The last week would be devoted to the Conference, to which scholars from universities across the country were being invited, ten or so of them to give papers.

The logistics, the fees, the programme had to be presented to Borges, ironed out, approved, and agreed by all parties. Alas, to complicate matters, Ivask had shuffled off to Málaga. I was now in the hands of Thomas Lyons, chairman of the Borges Conference Committee. Three months later, as he and I were nicely progressing, Lyons took up a post at the University of Wisconsin. I was then put in the hands of Jim Artman, of Oklahoma's Modern Languages Department.

Artman was one of those practical, down-to-earth Americans used to solving problems even before they raised their heads. In no time, he and I had the territory mapped out, including all the travel details and even the programme for Galen in New York. Borges and I managed as well to secure an invitation for our friend Murchison to deliver a paper for the Conference and to participate in the YM-YWHA poetry reading.

Was Elsa going to be bored and give trouble? If so, what trouble? Borges and I were on tenterhooks. We simply did not know.

In Buenos Aires on winter nights after work Borges and I would trudge in the dank chill from the Library to the Querandí for a cup of hot chocolate, a drink Georgie loved. The bar was a place attended by neighbourhood high-school students. One evening, while we were washing down the walls of the white urinal side by side, Borges asked if I spotted any interesting graffiti. There were scads, in pencil, ink, and marker pens of all colours, and each was filthier than the next. I read him one, a simple straightforward quatrain. For a moment or two he savoured the lines and pronounced them an excellent example of didactic verse. The matter rested there.

One day at the University of Oklahoma we were again lined up before the urinal, when Borges asked if I believed in cultural exchange.

'Of course,' I told him. 'Our trip here to Oklahoma is a perfect example of cultural exchange.'

'What I had in mind,' said Borges, 'was those didactic lines from the Querandí.'

I looked around me. The walls of this loo were pristine, not a mark on them. They were a pale pea-green and appeared to have been recently painted. But one was not going to deny Borges. I got out a pencil and wrote:

La mierda no es pintura,
el dedo no es pincel;
no sea hijo de puta,
límpiese con papel.

A rough-and-ready translation would be: Your shit is not housepaint, | your finger's not a brush; | don't be a stupid bastard, | wipe yourself with paper.

The next time we used the loo there was no trace of our verses. Someone at the University, to our deep disappointment, was not keen on cultural exchange.

We had been set up with an office. I posted on its door a schedule to indicate when Borges and I would be happy to make ourselves available to students. Not a single student ever took up our offer, so instead we used the office to continue our translating. While we were at work there, a revealing and useful thing happened. I had a copy of a new story by Borges but it was not one for which I'd yet prepared a draft in English. So the two of us waded in, working together straight from the Spanish original. All seemed to go well, and the story was accepted by *Harper's*.

I should mention that Borges and I shared from the

very outset the same views on translation. To us, words immediately suggested by the Spanish should be avoided in English. Spanish *oscuro* should not be translated as 'obscure' but as 'dark'; *habitación* should be 'room' and not 'habitation'. Words with Saxon roots were preferable to those of a Latinate origin. So far so good, but when in time *Harper's* sent a proof of the Borges story I could not believe what lay there under my eyes. The translation, so fraught with Saxon words, was utterly unreadable. I quickly cobbled together a new version and wrote back to the magazine, grovelling if I remember correctly, to use this one. I never mentioned the incident to Borges but there was a great lesson to be learned here. Ideas should never be carried to the point of absurdity, never become rigid. (To illustrate my point, the word *rígido* in Spanish should be translated not as 'rigid' but as 'stiff'.)

The staff at the Modern Languages Department could not have shown us more kindness. Thanksgiving Day fell during our visit, and one of the junior lecturers, Nick Mills, and his wife invited the four of us to share their turkey dinner. Elsa was glum and wore dark glasses while she ate her meal, but Borges was in a festive mood. He even partook in a session of clowning. I have a photo of him with a rakish napkin draped on his head, sticking out over his right ear from under an upside-down metallic bread basket worn like a hat. Georgie was not known for such shenanigans.

But there was constant irritation from Elsa's quarter that was spoiling the trip for Borges. She complained about everything. She had bouts of wild jealousy. Worst of all were the burning silent rages because Borges would not allow me to tell her how much we were paid for our readings. No, worst of all was the fact that the cheques were not being handed to her. I had glimpsed these eventualities from the day months earlier when I told her I too had been invited to Oklahoma. With me along, Borges had an ally, and she was not in sole control of him.

She insulted me at every turn, expressing unhappiness about the poor money this trip was netting her husband. This was remarkable because – apart from the Modern Language Department's fee – in one week reading poems Borges earned more than his salary for three months at the Library.

She was getting to me, and I could no longer hold back. She did nothing but lie, sulk, insult, and brag. I told Borges exactly what I thought of her.

'Yes,' he said, 'but she keeps telling me she's fond of me.'

I told him she only cared for his money.

He agreed. 'That's exactly what my mother thinks.' He also said that fond or not, Bioy had told him that Elsa was not making him happy.

One day she threatened to leave immediately for Argentina. I bet Borges that she wouldn't; he said he hoped she would. Of course, she backed down.

All our scheduled events went off like clockwork. So did the course of the Conference. Both Murchison and I, along with the distinguished Borges experts, gave papers. Lyons wrote from Wisconsin, asking us to give a poetry reading there. Incredibly, while at Oklahoma we also managed to work in readings at the University of Michigan, Michigan State, and the University of Texas. Later, from our base in New York, we squeezed in another at Georgetown University, in Washington.

At Austin, Borges could hardly wait to tear us away from the formal activities so that he could show me what he called 'the Tower of Blood'. This was the twenty-seven storey tower where in 1966 a lone, well-armed gunman had operated as a sniper and shot forty-eight people, fifteen of whom died, all in a span of ninety-six minutes. Beforehand he'd murdered his wife and mother. Charles Whitman, the killer, was an ex-Marine and an ex-altar boy. What staggered me was not the tower or the story but Borges's ghoulish, adolescent relish for the site.

On one of her shopping sprees in Norman, Elsa found herself in the university bookstore. She wanted a present for Georgie and aware of his interest in Old English bought for him, and wrote her signature in, a copy of Gower's *Confessio Amantis*. Alas, Gower is not Old but Middle English. Borges immediately went sniffy, handed the copy to me, and said, 'Keep it.'

At the Coronado Inn, where the University had put

us up, it was time to pack our bags for the plane to New York. We were driving to the airport at Oklahoma City, some twenty-three miles from Norman, in a limousine big enough for the four of us, our luggage, and Lowell Dunham and Jim Artman of the Modern Languages Department. We had driven quite a way, when suddenly there was a shocked whimper from Elsa, which startled us all. She announced that she had left her fur coat – her precious nutria *piel* – hanging behind the door of her hotel room.

A stunned silence reigned. Dunham reacted only to calm Elsa. He asked me for our New York address and said the University would send the coat on.

Was this the funniest night of my life? Or was it only funny in hindsight? Perhaps it was something else, a curious hybrid, a funny nightmare. I am going to try to tell it straight, just as it happened.

New York was a five-day endless round of activities – meetings, lunches, dinners, receptions, and cocktail parties. We arrived on 7 December and the next evening gave our reading for Galen at the Poetry Center. It was just Borges, Murchison, and me, and the programme consisted of new poems from *In Praise of Darkness*. This time the thousand-seat auditorium did not intimidate me.

As soon as we told Elsa that on the following night we were invited to a dinner party at the Rockefellers' she was off like a shot. She literally disappeared for the whole next day. The name Rockefeller had her entranced. I assumed – and was correct – that her disappearance was a tactical retreat to beautify herself.

She never asked which Rockefeller we were seeing. (It was Rodman – Nelson's thirty-seven-year-old son – and his wife.) Elsa probably did not know that the Rockefellers were a huge dynasty. Neither had she asked why the Rockefellers or what their connection was to us or ours to them. The connection was through their oil interests in South America and, on the cultural front, their support of the New York-based Center for Inter-American Relations, which was helping to subsidize Georgie and my translation activities.

Elsa could not contain herself as we arrived at the Rockefellers' Fifth Avenue flat. A lift brought us to their floor and opened directly into a foyer. Elsa was now wearing her back-up coat. As she stepped out of the lift – even before she stepped out of it – her eyes were swivelling in all directions in an attempt to take in everything she could at one go.

A liveried footman drew behind her, ready to take her coat. Elsa was oblivious of him. When the footman laid his hands on her shoulders in an effort to help peel off the garment, she pulled away as if foiling a thief. I was quickly by her side, whispering, 'Elsa, your coat.' She acceded but still her attention did not waver from what her gaze was drinking in.

She stepped into the drawing room, where Rodman and his wife came forward to greet her. She and Georgie were the evening's guests of honour. Rodman asked her if she'd care to see the flat. Here was her dream come true, and she breathed in deeply in preparation for the treat of a lifetime. I tagged along behind, thinking I might be needed for translation.

Elsa was absolutely beside herself. She pulled a small Kodak out of her handbag and began diligently to photograph the interior of the house. She asked Mrs Rockefeller to sit on the bed while she took a picture of the bedroom. Putting her hands on Mrs Rockefeller's dress, Elsa said, 'And what is this, Mrs Rockefeller?'

'That's silk, Mrs Borges.'

Hands on again. 'And what is this, Mrs Rockefeller?'

'That's wool, Mrs Borges.'

When she photographed the bathroom she got another guest to sit on the toilet.

Mr Rockefeller looked on.

'And what is this, Mr Rockefeller?' Elsa continued.

He told her.

'And what is this, Mr Rockefeller?' she asked at the next opportunity.

He told her.

On and on it went. Elsa pointing, Rodman Rockefeller explaining. Each time she indicated, let me make it clear, she was not pointing to a painting, a drawing, a tapestry, or a work of art of any kind. In the loo, she pointed to a soap dish, a hand towel. She was mesmerized. And there I was, trailing behind, holding my breath and dying a thousand deaths. All the others were doing their utmost not to notice her.

The tour ended, I gulped down a drink and circulated. From here on Elsa could fend for herself. At this point, one of the party, whom I had just met, leaned to me and said, 'Where did he ever get this low-class bitch?'

I was more shocked by his words than by the vulgar spectacle Elsa was making of herself. I was used to her behaviour but I was not used to ice-water words like this man's being thrown into my face. My god, I told myself, everyone else has her measure too.

At last we were ushered into the dining room, where a long, richly laid oval table awaited us. The hosts were meticulous. They held in their hands a small cardboard layout of the table, with little tabs for the name of each guest.

Rodman came round to one end of the table, laid a hand on it, and announced that the guest of honour, Jorge Luis Borges, would sit there. Georgie no sooner heard the host's words than he panicked and threw himself down in the nearest chair. 'No,' he announced, 'I'll just sit here.'

The Rockefellers were nonplussed. They began plucking out the tabs and resetting them round their imaginary table. Meanwhile, an Uruguayan sculptor by the name of Gonzalo Fonseca plumped down to stake his claim for what was meant to be Georgie's place. I liked Fonseca's no-nonsense, democratic style and was fast to take the seat to his immediate left. This got the Rockefellers into another tizzy, and the tabs were plucked out and reset a second time. In the end the hosts gave up and let their guests sit where they chose. Resigned, Rodman took his place opposite Fonseca at the far end of the table.

A footman – maybe it was the same one who'd had to struggle to strip off Elsa's coat – made his rounds of the table dribbling out tiny portions of wine. When he came around to Fonseca for the second time, Gonzalo seized the man's hand and held it over his glass to see that he received a decent portion. On the footman's third circumnavigation Gonzalo courteously accepted the dribble. The footman then carried the bottle to a table to one side of the room. No sooner had he set the bottle down than Gonzalo sprang into action. The footman tried to defend his territory, but he and Gonzalo were quickly locked in a silent tug-of-war.

To avoid a scene the footman gave in and Gonzalo returned to his place at the table, where he ostentatiously set the bottle down. 'I'm used to drinking a litre of wine with my meals,' he said, turning to me. I was delighted. Fonseca's antics had gone a long way to mitigating Elsa's.

Before the night was over Elsa had managed to buttonhole Rockefeller to ask for his help in getting her suitcases through customs. She told him she had bought a lot of clothing and was taking it back to Buenos Aires in aid of charities. The rest of us sat frozen and speechless. The latter part of her claim, Borges later told me, was an outright lie. She was bringing the stuff back to sell.

Emerging from our taxi on the way home to the flat that our publishers had lent us, Elsa's face still had its dreamy look and in her eyes the stars still sparkled.

18   New York and the Fur Coat

We were in New York for the rest of that week. At the end of it, Heather and I went up to New England to visit our families, while Georgie and Elsa returned to Buenos Aires.

Meanwhile, to Elsa's galloping chagrin, the nutria had gone to ground somewhere between Norman and New York. This predicament possessed and obsessed her. She hardly left Borges alone, with worry and with a disgust for his inaction. I could only tell her that the coat would turn up and that our publisher would send it round to her consulate, which would put the poor beleaguered fur onto an Argentine flight.

A few days later, attending our last New York event, a cocktail party given by the consulate, Elsa went into action. She cornered – literally – the Argentine ambassador and filled him in at length on what had happened to her coat and on the failed promises of the University of Oklahoma. The ambassador nodded and nodded but could not work himself out from her clutches. Two or three times he promised her that the moment her fur arrived in New

York he would see that it reached the consulate and from there made its way to an aeroplane.

While this went on, Georgie sat in another corner of the room being badgered by someone in publishing who wanted him to write an article for him. Naturally, Borges agreed.

The ambassador caught my eye and approached me across the room. Nodding his head in the direction of Elsa, he whispered, 'Di Giovanni, I feel sympathy for you.'

Elsa liked nothing better than rubbing shoulders and getting chummy with Argentine diplomatic officials. The ambassador must have given her a shred of hope and comfort, because she immediately relaxed and freely partook of, or freely stuffed herself on, all the rich foods the party could offer. As a result, she spent the last day of her New York visit in bed, at death's door, suffering from a liver complaint. It wasn't until an hour before take-off that we knew whether or not she would be able to leave the country.

Let us summarize. Elsa left her fur coat behind in Oklahoma and Borges's overcoat behind in New York. Two books on Persian mysticism that a publisher made Borges gifts of she jettisoned. In this way she had room to carry back her own new wardrobe and trinkets.

19   Buenos Aires and the Fur Coat

The nutria (*Myocastor coypus*) is a rodent the size of a beaver that inhabits burrows in Argentine riverbanks. A prolific breeder, it is hunted and trapped for its fur. It is also known as the 'river rat' and 'coypu'. The animal has a rat-like tail, long whiskers, and large orange-yellow incisors. It can grow up to twenty pounds in weight and twenty-four inches in length. Its shaggy fur is frankly unappealing but it has a soft underfur ranging from dark to yellowish brown. This is the fur that is employed in the manufacture of garments, and it was this undercoat that was used to make Elsa's *piel*.

The non-appearance in Buenos Aires of her personal nutria had immediate repercussions. I had no sooner set foot back in the city than Borges phoned to say that Elsa did not want me coming round to the house any more.

'What's going on?' I asked.

'Meet me at the Library and I'll tell you.'

'Are we going to be able to continue our work?'

'Of course,' Borges said.

At the Biblioteca Nacional he told me that the fur coat

still had not arrived and that Elsa was accusing me of having stolen it.

Nothing could have been more absurd. 'What would I want with her fur coat?' I said.

'No, di Giovanni,' Borges was quick to reply. 'You haven't stolen her fur coat because you're not a thief.'

There was obviously more to her banishment of me than the coat; the nutria was just a handy excuse. In her eyes she had lost control of her husband because of me. The last thing that interested Elsa was the work Borges and I were doing. The fact that, influenced by me and our successes abroad, he was writing again, beginning to publish new books after years in the creative doldrums, meant nothing to her.

The way Borges was able to confide in me released some of the pressure on him from her quarter and somehow allowed him to make excuses for her. 'She's just a child,' he told me. 'She can't get along without me.'

He was dragging his feet, deluding himself. I had told him he must shed Elsa; so had doña Leonor, whom I was visiting more and more frequently. She too despaired for her son. 'The trouble is,' she told me, '*Georgie no tiene carácter.*' Georgie has no backbone. Still Borges could not face making the break. And yet he authorized me to open an account in his name in a New York bank, where I was secretly to deposit all his income from *The New Yorker*.

At any rate, he stood up to Elsa about me and quickly

established that I should still come round to the Belgrano flat to pick him up in the afternoons, but, unfortunately, I would have to wait for him outside the house. I didn't mind. What I didn't want to lose were our long leisurely walks to the Library. On these promenades we were able to talk over plans uninterrupted, and I could fill him in on our progress with *The New Yorker* and other magazines as well as with our book publishers. The distance of ten or so blocks also gave us a chance to gossip, for – as the story I am telling here should have made clear by now – Borges was a consummate gossiper.

We would begin our stroll down the Avenida Belgrano, a wide, busy, modern thoroughfare, trying to speak over the roar and fumes of the traffic. The ubiquitous snub-nosed buses crawled along in step with us, throbbing and belching their murderous black exhaust in our faces. Borges never seemed to notice. He was too busy discussing the word music of Dunbar, Coleridge, or the Bard himself, whose 'multitudinous seas incarnadine', capped with 'making the green one red', never failed to rouse and thrill him. Strangely, he misunderstood the words 'making the green one red'. He once said to me, 'Look, di Giovanni, Shakespeare has personified the sea.' Borges was reading it, 'making the Green One red'.

The avenue had been built in fairly recent times during a programme of street widening, which meant the demolition of houses on either side of the earlier roadway. Parallel to the avenue, two streets to the south, was Calle México, and there, between Bolívar and Perú, stood the National Library.

To escape the bothersome traffic we had the choice of crossing Belgrano and cutting south either one block to Venezuela or two to México. These streets might be lined tight with parked cars but they were relatively peaceful. There was a stretch of México that consisted of old-fashioned two-storey buildings with balconies that teemed with people, plants, and drying clothes that were draped over their balustrades. The buildings might have been boarding houses. Across their fronts ran untidy ropes of electric and telephone cables. It was a humble neighbourhood of rundown shops and dingy bars.

In the immediate vicinity of the Library industrial goods such as heavy-duty pumps were displayed in the shop windows. The only trouble with making our way on these back streets was the narrowness of the pavements; the two of us could not comfortably walk abreast, which meant that with Borges clinging to my arm I had to proceed half a step ahead of him in a crabwise manner.

It was among these homely streets one afternoon that Borges had a sudden accident with his bladder. All at once his grip on my arm tightened and I recognized the panic in his face. He had pursed his lips as if trying to hold something back. I scanned the street for a bar and at last spotted one.

'I'm not going to make it,' he said.

'Hold on, it's just here.'

The toilets in Buenos Aires bars are always at the far rear. The passageway leading to this one was quite narrow. Borges stuck his arms out ahead of him like a sleepwalker, the crook of his stick hooked over the bend of his elbow. He was wearing a grey tweed suit. The onlookers in the bar shifted themselves out of his path as he hurtled along. But it was too late. Urine was gushing in a heavy stream down his legs inside his trousers and squishing over the sides of his shoes. He made it to the urinal, but by this time his socks and shoes and tweed trousers were urine-soaked.

When we emerged onto the street, I said, 'We'd better go back to the house for you to change.'

'No, we'll go on,' he said. 'This is just an illusion.'

There were footprints of urine along the bar's tiled floor, but the clientele all looked aside and pretended not to notice.

It was in the course of these daily walks that Borges gossiped to me about all and sundry – and it was not always benign. One day it was the turn of novelist Ernesto Sabato, whom Georgie dubbed the Dostoyevsky of Santos Lugares (the out-of-town suburb where Sabato lived) for his bouts of melancholy. Borges chuckled over a story told in solemn seriousness by Ernesto's wife Matilde. She had accompanied her husband on a flight to the interior, where Sabato was due to give a talk. When the plane landed it became Matilde's painful duty to inform the puzzled reception committee not to approach her husband. 'Ernesto,' she told them, '*está en un pozo de melancolía.*' Ernesto's in a pit of melancholy.

I got my oar in. I told Borges about the time I was strolling down Calle Florida with Ernesto and Matilde. Matilde was proselytizing me. To prove her husband's worth and standing as a novelist she drew from her handbag a sheaf of reviews, some in French, and began reading them aloud to me.

Georgie might have a go at Victoria Ocampo, 'Queen Victoria', belittling her for her ignorance of printing procedures. He said she would ask why, when space at the end of some page or other of *Sur* had to be filled, they couldn't just stretch lines of type as if they were made of rubber. I suspect that Borges as a young man had been very much in awe of Victoria and her imperious and dashing bohemian ways. Perhaps he'd had a secret crush on her. She was rich, aristocratic, chic, exotic. She had taken the writer Eduardo Mallea, some thirteen years younger than herself, as a lover. Mallea became a novelist with an international reputation while Borges was struggling to write his difficult early stories. Mallea's reputation eventually went into steady decline; Borges's grew. Mallea used to invite me to tea in cafés along Corrientes to express his total admiration for Borges and his work. All Georgie ever said to me about Mallea was that he had a touch of the tarbrush.

At the Library we shuffled through the revolving-door entrance and up the grand marble staircase, entering first Borges's outer office with its scruffy, bare, wooden floor. It was here that the secretaries huddled at a tiny table in a corner by a window. Except next to that window, the room was lightless, bleak, and spartan. A small wire wastebasket stood beside the table. There was one telephone – big, clumsy, black, its cord frayed. It didn't matter. The phones, like the secretaries, only worked part-time.

The building dated from 1901 and had been, as Borges was fond of telling visitors, the seat of the national lottery. On the stairway, replicas of the lottery balls were worked into the balustrade. Borges would tap them with his stick. The inner sanctum, his office, had a very high ceiling, green wallpaper printed with bamboo-like fronds, polished mahogany panelling, and a parquet floor. We worked at a massive old-fashioned conference table in the centre of the room. At the far end was the desk that Paul Groussac, a distinguished predecessor who also ended up blind, had had built to his own design. It was U-shaped, with strange drawers and odd compartments. If you sat behind it as Borges never did, the desk surrounded you. There was something both gloomy and sinister about such a piece of furniture.

The room's other furnishings were a couple of revolving bookshelves and a tall set of drawers where Borges slipped the drafts of poems he dictated in the mornings to one of the secretaries. Two pairs of doors led off the room straight onto a corridor. These we used only when trying to avoid someone who might be waiting in the outer office or when we went to the vast, stark loo that was used only by us. Sometimes Borges, who was shy about his false teeth, would take them out here to rinse and would say to me, 'Don't look now.'

Next door was the room Groussac had died in, a detail Borges took ghoulish delight in recounting, for once upon a time the director had lived on the premises. There were traces of a kitchen that proved it. But Elsa would not hear of making a home in the Library. It was a gloomy place, and there were times when I thought I too would go blind there.

On the main table where we worked lay a dictionary of the Spanish Royal Academy, the smell of whose paper and binding Borges and I were fond of savouring.

In the outer office visitors waited to be announced by a secretary. One day the secretary told Borges that Jean de Milleret was there to see him. Milleret was a Frenchman who lived in Buenos Aires and was well known to Borges. He had conducted a book-length interview with Borges in French, and the volume, *Entretiens avec Jorge Luis Borges*, was published in Paris in 1967. Now the book had been translated into Spanish and had appeared in Buenos Aires.

In an uncharacteristic outburst Borges came near to shouting. 'I don't want to see him; tell him to go away.'

When he had calmed down a bit, I said, 'What was that all about? Didn't you do a book of interviews with him?'

'Yes,' said Borges.

'And?'

'Well, he made me say unfriendly things about my family,' Borges said.

'Made you say? Did you say those things or not?'

Borges went sheepish. 'Well, yes, but I never thought the book would make its way back to Buenos Aires.'

The secretary came in to say that Milleret had left. She placed on the table a copy of the interviews in French, with numerous inked in corrections, that Milleret had been there to deliver. On the half-title page he had written the words, '*Au Maître d'oeuvre en témoignage d'estime, de compréhension et d'amitié.*' What about the Master's esteem, understanding, and friendship for the Frenchman? Evaporated without a trace due to no fault of Milleret.

Borges handed the book to me. 'You have it,' he said.

The one place in all Buenos Aires where my tweed suit was no match for the winter was in the dank cavern of Borges's office. There was a large ornate fireplace at my back, where flameless eucalyptus logs would glow – not burn but glow. If I backed up to them now and again, the icy chill was momentarily dispelled. As Borges used to say, one was grateful for small mercies.

Sometimes Borges and I wandered around in the Library's basement stacks in search of a book. The place teemed with cats, whose job it was to keep down the mouse population. They did, but the price was an overpowering stench of feline urine.

We might turn a corner of this labyrinth of shelves and surprise a small knot of employees who were gathered round drinking maté. When they saw it was Borges – or even me if I were alone – they lost no time bowing and scraping. Their embarrassed actions suggested they were doing something illicit but, if they were, Borges could not have cared less. Here underground the Library's books were arranged by their size, not subject, in order to have uniform shelf heights. So a book on geometry might rub shoulders with a volume of Virgil or a French poet or a treatise on Celtic mysteries – so long as all three measured the same height.

These vaults were not without their occasional bookish adventures. Late one afternoon the sky went black, and there was a calamitous thunderstorm such as those you never see anywhere but in Buenos Aires. In the blink of an eye the streets were swollen rivers. This storm was accompanied by a power failure, so that suddenly we were without electric light. After a time, when the rain had abated, everyone – readers and staff – left the building. Borges and I needed a volume of Victor Hugo in order to finish an article for *The Book of Imaginary Beings*. The watchman lent us a weak torch that allowed us to prowl the stacks looking for Hugo's poems. Victor Hugo might have been anywhere among the Library's holding of 800,000 volumes, but Borges and I were not deterred. We started out in the dark in search of our book. Something made us inch through the first-floor stacks and start for the next level. Ahead of us the stairway split, one branch curving round to the right and the other to the left. Something impelled me to the left. When we reached the head of the stairs I was forced to pause for Borges, half a step behind me, to catch up. As I did so, the beam of my light came to rest on a set of Hugo's complete works.

'Isn't this a stroke of luck?' I said.

'I think we'd best be leaving with our book now,' Borges answered. 'The word for this is uncanny.'

A door or two away along Mexico Street from the Library was the headquarters of the Association of Argentine Writers, always referred to by its Spanish acronym, SADE. Its building was one of the city's few structures still standing that dated back to colonial times. This made it a favourite of Borges's. A single storey tall, it had a flat roof with a masonry balustrade on the street side like the kind Borges's artist sister Norah was fond of depicting. You entered it from the street through a wide arched doorway called a *zaguán*. A coach and horses would once have driven in and out of here. The driveway led a long distance straight through into the interior of the house, and along it were a series of patios, usually three, onto which the rooms, with their galleries, opened. The first patio had a well head to hoist water from the cistern below. Throughout the house the windows were grilled. Servants were housed at the rear, and grape arbours shaded the patios. Borges had often written about these black-and-white chequerboard-tiled patios. The place had a welcome sleepy peacefulness about it. Some Spanish documentary film-makers once shot Borges here in one of the rooms, rocking back and forth in an old chair.

It was to a front room of this building that Borges asked me to accompany him on a certain winter's morning. The occasion was the wake of his one-time close friend, the poet and novelist Leopoldo Marechal, from whom he had been estranged for many years. Marechal had published a novel in 1948, *Adán Buenosayres*, in which Borges figured as one of the protagonists. But the split with Marechal was not over that and had taken place considerable years earlier. Alas, they had fallen out over the issue of Peronism.

Marechal looked small lying there in his open coffin. Borges stood by the side of the corpse, contemplative, for several minutes. He then made his way to speak a few words with one of Marechal's daughters. When we left and were back out on Mexico Street I could see that Borges had been moved and was distressed and saddened to see the dead man. It seemed to be one more instance of the long shadow of Perón come to haunt him.

Borges's secretaries were friendly and loyal. They were unfailingly considerate of me because they knew that we were all on the same side – Borges's. They were serious in their work, unpretentious in their manner, and probably not highly educated. One of them entered the office one morning, and it was obvious that she had been crying. She had come to tell Borges about the *cadete*. The word *cadete* in the lingo of Buenos Aires meant a messenger boy, an errand boy. Every office had one. They usually wore some kind of uniform.

The Library's particular *cadete* was a small man, brown as a nut, with receding hair. He was serious and unfailingly polite. I think he was much younger than he looked. The secretary wanted to tell us that after an absence of four or five days, the *cadete* had died the night before. This was unimaginable, for the man had always seemed in good health.

'You see,' the secretary explained, 'he lived in a *villa miseria* on the outskirts of town. His tin shack had no running water or proper sewage. He had a family, and what with payments on a television, a refrigerator, and so on, he had worn himself out trying to make ends meet.'

Borges turned to me after the secretary left the room. His voice had a register of sympathy in it that I seldom heard from him.

'Look at that, di Giovanni. The poor fellow was paying for a refrigerator and television. I don't understand why the working man isn't content just to read his Shakespeare or his Dante.'

It was always a source of amazement to me how little Borges was able to understand the lives of ordinary people – how infrequently he emerged from his shell to show sympathy with others. We knew a poet named Arturo Cuadrado, an exile from fascist Spain. Along with many of the Spanish Republican fraternity, Cuadrado haunted the Avenida de Mayo, and every once in a while Borges and I ran into him on the street. Because of Borges's blindness, Arturo would approach and always introduce himself in this way: '*Soy yo, el poeta, el español.*' It's me, the poet, the Spaniard. There was a gentle sweetness about this, and the words never failed to amuse Borges. He often repeated them to me, not cruelly but in fun, slightly mocking Cuadrado's tone of Spanish pride and including the Spanish lisp in the last word. One day on the Avenida Cuadrado approached, all sadness and despondency. He told Borges he'd just had news that his mother had died in Spain. When Arturo left us, Borges turned to me and said, 'You see, di Giovanni, to us he was always an object of fun, but here he is now, a flesh-and-blood man suffering.'

But what about Elsa's fur coat? Over the weeks since our return from New York she had hounded and hounded Borges. What was he going to do about it? Georgie never lifted a finger over anything, and Elsa knew it. She was the 'logical' one, and she took every opportunity to get the boot in. Then one day she decided to take matters into her own hands.

Without a word to Borges she went straight to the American Embassy and asked to see the ambassador. John Davis Lodge, the ambassador, had only recently arrived in Buenos Aires. Official procedure, protocol, was that he would soon formally invite Borges to the embassy to make the distinguished writer's acquaintance. But Lodge had not worked round to this yet, and here was Elsa at his door asking for an audience. He could not refuse her.

Of course she recounted to him the history – maybe even the pre-history – of the missing nutria fur coat. No doubt she was meticulous, painstaking, in her story. Ambassador Lodge could only have thanked her for the visit and pledged to look into her case.

The moment she left – I got this bit of the tale from the American cultural attaché – Lodge was beside himself with anger. 'I never want to lay eyes on that woman again,' he shouted to his staff. 'Under no circumstances is she ever to be allowed to set foot through my door.'

Weeks and weeks passed and still no sighting of the homeless nutria. Had Lodge initiated inquiries? As we had no inkling of Elsa's visit to him, Georgie and I remained in the dark.

Then one day the cultural attaché phoned me to say that the fur coat had been retrieved. I could come and pick it up at the embassy. A fee, no doubt exacted by Argentine customs officials, had been paid by the embassy and they asked for reimbursement.

But where had the errant nutria been all this time? I wanted to know. Only then was I let in on what for months had been a hush-hush saga. Members of the Argentine consulate in New York, together with officials of the Argentine national airlines, had conspired to smuggle goods into the country. Over a long period, on the arrival of the suspect planes, anything on them – everything on them, including stray nutria fur coats – had been impounded in a bonded warehouse to be used as evidence against the ring of contrabandists.

So Elsa had her *piel* back, and her long, long grievance had come to a satisfactory conclusion. Was I forgiven for the alleged theft? No.

Just as well, thought I. Best let sleeping dogs, or in this case bitches, lie. As for Borges he repaid me the fee I'd paid the embassy but of the whole botched affair and the outcome he had not a word to say. He was quietly biding his time.

20   Silent Sufferer

It was not Borges's style, his upbringing, to complain or
or to make a fuss or to put on a display of martyrdom.
Wallowing in self-pity, as he termed it, he found abhorrent.
Thus he simply accustomed himself to Elsa's abuse and in
the main ignored it. But the truth is that he was engaged
in domestic civil war, in conjugal torture, and he thought
it best, as much as he was able, to keep these troubles to
himself. Although Elsa was now out of my life, Borges
continued to supply me with a steady flow of news about
her. His tales were always understated and he tried to
relate them with amusement, but nothing could disguise
his underlying despair.

Following our return from New York, we had buried
ourselves in work. Mornings Borges dictated stories that
would become *El informe de Brodie*. Afternoons we
polished drafts for our volume *The Aleph and Other Stories*.
I could measure just how unhappy he was by the plain fact
that he kept away all he could from the Belgrano flat.

One skirmish in the ongoing civil war involved Elsa's

son Ricardo. He was out of work and she wanted Georgie as a state employee and a figure of some standing – he was after all director of the Argentine National Library – to use his position to land Ricardo a job. The notion struck Borges as nepotism, and he could not stomach it. Elsa was incensed. Perhaps, forced to give in, Borges had turned to Edmundo Clemente, his very capable assistant director, to deal with the problem. In the end, whoever initiated it, the stratagem succeeded. Ricardo had employment as a kind of courier to make the rounds and collect the takings from shops that sold lottery tickets.

I suppose it was in a last desperate effort to mend fences that Borges roped Elsa into helping him with a commission to translate Walt Whitman's *Leaves of Grass*. Elsa knew no English. It was fingernails on the blackboard for Borges to endure her difficulty in attempting to pronounce English and read him Whitman's verses. The project turned out a colossal misjudgement on Borges's part. The publisher's editor called me to her home to point out the deficiencies in the script. Whole lines had been omitted or glossed over for no apparent reason. It seemed that whenever Borges found words or a phrase he did not grasp he skirted them. There was a sloppiness, a carelessness, in the presentation that one would never have guessed of him. From the casual remarks Borges made to me about Elsa's editorial incapacity I knew that somewhere along the line the translation for him had turned into a piece of hackwork. The unlucky editor was ultimately forced to save the day by sitting down and devoting hours and hours with Borges to make the translation presentable.

As the weeks drew on I noticed that we had begun to lose working days when Borges simply could not settle in. He might use a touch of humour to tip me off that he could not concentrate, which I knew to mean that problems with Elsa had flared up again. In a jaunty voice he would say to me, 'I suppose you're thinking of Marichal all the time.' I was not thinking of Marichal or Harvard or Cambridge any of the time. Borges's remark was double-edged. It hinted to me that we would not get any work done that day and it was also a sly dig at Marichal. Instead of knuckling down into what we had to do, Borges would ask me to read him a Kipling story.

On another occasion we would be working well, when suddenly his thoughts would fly off. Then, returning to himself, he would say something fairly benign or neutral about Elsa. Whatever touched it off, his reverie might hark back to their days together in Cambridge. 'She kept asking me to dedicate a poem to her,' Borges once said. 'I didn't want to but she insisted and insisted. In the end I found it easier just to be done with it. Fourteen lines, a sonnet. It took me all of ten minutes to write.' The last had been uttered with a sneer.

One day a secretary ushered into the office an American visitor. She was a slightly older woman, elegant and smartly dressed. She said she was from Grolier's, the New York encyclopedia publishers, and had come to discuss the article Borges had agreed to write for them. Borges began to squirm. Suddenly he flared up and spoke some uncalled-for harsh words. He then sprang to his feet and slipped out of the double doors to the loo.

I asked the woman, Janet Stone, what on earth had so provoked him. What was this article he promised to write? It turned out that she and Borges had never spoken before the present encounter, but at a year-end party given by the Argentine consulate in New York Borges had agreed with one of her colleagues to write something for them. I then remembered the man – he was a Latin American – and he had badgered the life out of Borges in a corner of the room. Borges had agreed to write a short history of Argentina, Mrs Stone told me. My heart dropped down into my shoes. Here was Borges, up to his old tricks again. His way of dismissing the man was to give in to him. Our schedules, plus our difficulties, did not permit of even a two-word piece on Argentine history. Mrs Stone, however, struck me as a kind, intelligent person to whom things like this should never happen. I suppose I felt guilty on Borges's behalf. 'Go now, and don't press him,' I counselled her. I asked where she was staying – it was at the Plaza Hotel – and I mumbled that I would try to work something out.

When Borges returned from his Old Norse I told him he had treated the poor woman outrageously. He seemed to agree and, calm now, he said he had promised what the man asked for because after all it was New York and the next day he was travelling back to Buenos Aires. As if Buenos Aires made him invisible and shielded him from being tracked down.

'But you gave your word,' I said. 'They were acting in good faith, and you lied.'

I was particularly pressing him because I knew of two other instances of this same behaviour on his part. Within days of Borges's departure from Cambridge, Murchison had received a letter from an editor at the University of Chicago Press. 'It has been over a year now,' the man wrote, 'since we sent off to you the transcript of Sr. Borges's lecture, "Walt Whitman, the Man and the Myth". Although I wrote to Sr. Borges several times last spring, and sent him a cable last July, I have had no response from him.'

I myself had got entangled in Borges's unwillingness to deal with his Norton lectures for the Harvard University Press. He had simply left the Press hanging when he omitted to send them a text of the talks. Ann Louise Coffin, a friend of mine at the HUP, had been forced to write to me to say that the Press was 'anxious to learn how Sr. Borges is coming on with the manuscript' of the lectures. 'But we've had no word these past two years.'

Alas, I'd had to inform her that Borges was doing nothing about the lectures. I added that I didn't think he was keen about shaping them for publication, and the excuse I made was that he felt his lectures were given extemporaneously and that to prepare them for publication would mean writing them from scratch.

What I was not revealing was that to prepare the lectures for publication would have forced Borges into reliving his unpleasant Cambridge days alongside Elsa. My guess was that he felt the talks he delivered he had delivered and that that was an end to the matter. I regarded his lapse as irresponsible, just as I now regarded his treatment of Mrs Stone.

In the end, I became the badgerer. I told Borges we simply had to get someone else to write the Grolier article. Glad of a way out, Borges contacted his old friend the historian José Luis Lanuza. Lanuza was doubly flattered. He had a commission from a New York publisher and he had been recommended to them by none other than Borges. So far so good for Lanuza, Borges, and Stone.

Grolier now pressed me. Could I not get Borges to write an introduction to Lanuza's contribution? They were offering a healthy fee of $1,000 for 1,500 words. But only I knew what it was going to take to get 1,500 words out of Borges in the present climate. I wrote back to them that the deal was on but the terms would be $1,500 dollars for 1,000 words. By now Mrs Stone and I were friends. She agreed.

Then a curious thing happened. In the middle of April 1970 there was a kidnap threat on Borges, and for a whole week a policeman tagged along beside him. Borges, of course, was much amused.

Elsa, Elsa, Elsa. As mentioned, I had neither spoken to nor laid eyes on her since we parted in New York. But I was becoming frantic about the way that even at a distance she kept interrupting our work. One morning back in Cambridge when his misery concerning his wife was written all over his face, I had asked Borges why on earth he'd ever married her.

He went pensive, searching for an adequate answer. After a longish pause he said, 'We had known each other when we were young. Then decades passed without our seeing any more of each other. A few years ago we met again. I thought here we are meeting again. This is destiny.'

'You mean you were thinking of cyclical time and the eternal return,' I said. These were two complicated philosophical concepts that had long intrigued Borges.

'Yes, that's it,' Borges said.

'But, Borges,' I told him, 'don't you see that you've fallen into one of your own literary traps?'

'Yes, I suppose I have,' he said sadly.

In these trying days during the southern hemisphere autumn of 1970 there were nonetheless a couple of high points. I had finished work on his 1940 story 'The Circular Ruins', an indisputable masterpiece of his. As was our custom, once we regarded a translation finished I would read him the English version straight through without any reference to the original. On this occasion I had his total attention. He fell into one of his frequent habits, which was to wrap his handkerchief round his right index finger and with it trace out a writing motion on the surface of the table. He was composing his story again. I finished my reading. '*Caramba*,' said Borges, his voice gone strange, 'I wish I could still write like that.' In his eyes there were tears.

The other high point was the beginning of our three-month marathon to set down directly in English his autobiography. This had been a pet idea of mine to enhance our volume *The Aleph and Other Stories*. I had asked the modern languages people at Oklahoma to transcribe for us Borges's lecture on himself delivered back at the beginning of December. When the nineteen- or twenty-page script arrived, I quickly perused it and discovered that with Borges's having jumped wildly from topic to topic the talk was incoherent and therefore useless. Screwing up my courage, I told him so. And I got one of his astonishing replies. 'Fling it aside and be free,' he said. 'We'll begin again from scratch.'

Nearly three weeks to the day into drafting the first pages of the autobiography, we were busy at work when apropos of nothing Borges suddenly said, referring to his marriage to Elsa and surfacing from a deep thought, 'I've committed what seems to me now an unaccountable mistake, a huge mistake – a quite unexplainable and mysterious mistake.'

21   An Aside

That last extraordinary sentence is worth repeating and analysing.

'I've committed what seems to me now an unaccountable mistake, a huge mistake – a quite unexplainable and mysterious mistake.'

The first thing to note about this statement is the wording – its measured structure, the rhetorical repetitions of the word 'mistake' three times and the four modifying adjectives. Even in the pit of despair Borges could not help but express himself in a formal literary way.

The second and more important thing to notice is the taint in the words of ongoing, unconscious self-delusion. Has Borges only at this point, after all he has been through, wakened to his mistake? Of the four adjectives to define it only the word 'huge' is indisputable. But 'unaccountable'? Given his literary fantasies and musings and his mother's relentless manoeuvrings, the mistake is all too accountable. 'Unexplainable'? Again, all too explainable. Borges is still abdicating responsibility for the mistake.

For one thing, the statement is a reflection of Borges's inability to account for reality. Had he not been invited to Harvard he wouldn't have needed to get married. Even then, why hadn't anyone in his closed circle come up with a more sensible and feasible plan – especially since the issue of the bed would not have reared its ugly head. He could have hired a suitable companion to look after him and to accompany him to Cambridge.

According to Fani, doña Leonor's maid, Borges's mother had taken Elsa aside before the wedding ceremony and told her, 'Listen, Georgie is not going to want to share his bed.' To which Elsa arrogantly replied – using the same words she had spoken to me in Cambridge – 'I know how to take a man to bed.' Self-delusion on her part too.

Borges's self-knowledge and common sense, if he possessed either of them, seem to have abandoned him. Given his long history of sexual failure with women, what made him think that, having evaded marriage for sixty-eight years, a late matrimonial relationship was now going to blossom and thrive?

Painful recollections must have been constantly intruding on him despite his best efforts to achieve the duty to happiness that he frequently spoke of. He had experienced so much disappointment in his life that he became inured to it. He had accepted his lot. He was resigned, fatalistic. At one point he even delved into the tenets of Buddhism to make palatable his self-disgust with an ageing and decaying body. Quite often he regarded the unpleasant or distressing events of life as illusory and therefore unworthy of discussion. Remember the incident of his bladder and the tweed suit. I wonder if, despite the public image of himself that he cultivated, the exterior of cheer and simplicity he put on to charm people, Borges did not suffer from chronic depression.

Nonetheless, to me the statement quoted above marked the turning point. What hitherto Borges had kept close to his chest he was now bringing out into the open. It was the beginning of an end to the unprofitable silence.

Secretly, almost imperceptibly, there was a shift, a slow change of attitude.

Carlos Fernández Ordóñez, a lawyer from the bordering Province of Córdoba, dropped in at the Library. He had a daughter who lived in Buenos Aires and he wrote poems, sonnets mostly, that Borges judged good enough to take to *La Nación* to get them published.

Fernández Ordóñez was a big man, a massive man. He had thick lips and his girth commenced at his neck. In his middle and on down to his thighs he was of inordinate proportions. It was plain that the man liked to eat. How long he and Borges had been friends I do not know, but he was loyal and of his devotion to Borges there was no question.

He also had literary taste and was an assiduous reader of Proust. Fernández Ordóñez even named his daughter Solange, after one of the French master's characters. He once informed me of, or explained, a valuable truth about life in Argentina. It was something I myself had experienced but had never managed to articulate.

'What's the most forlorn moment of the week?' he had said. And his answer was, 'Sunday afternoon.' Yes, those Sunday afternoons in Buenos Aires, not a soul on the dreary streets, always struck me as yawning and empty and as if time stood still. In a provincial place like Córdoba it must have been a hundred times worse.

There was another little story that Fernández Ordóñez told me, this one more exclusively concerning himself. It too had a truth about it, but at the same time it was amusing. As a big man with a big appetite it followed that he looked forward to his Sunday afternoon siestas. When they seemed to drag on beyond a reasonable limit, his wife would call out to him, 'Carlos, wake up. What are you doing?' But Carlos was already awake sitting on the edge of the bed, his feet planted on the floor. 'I'm resting from my siesta,' he would announce grumpily.

Borges, in a turmoil concerning the fortunes of his home wars, had told me in advance that Fernández Ordóñez was going to pay him a visit at the Library. I suggested that this opportunity be used to explore the possibilities of a divorce. For days Borges had been expressing doubts and scepticism over the feasibility of a legal split with Elsa. I knew, however, that he was just airing his ingrained fatalism. When the lawyer appeared, I made myself scarce.

We resumed work at the Library at five the next afternoon. Borges plunged in, and I could see his ploy was to concentrate hard so as to avert any questioning on my part about what had transpired on the previous evening between him and Fernández Ordóñez.

You cannot sit across from someone day in and day out for long, intense periods without being able to read every nuance of their speech, every quirk of their body language, every last one of their evasions.

'How did it go with Fernández Ordóñez?' I asked.

Borges appeared stricken, as if a last hope had been dashed, and he did not want to reply.

'What did he say?' I pressed. 'What did you tell him?'

'He wasn't very encouraging,' Borges said.

'Did you mention divorce?'

'He didn't think it possible.'

'But what did you say to him? Did you tell him about her behaviour that night at the Rockefellers'? Did you tell him how she alienated you from your colleagues at Harvard? Did you tell him how she interferes with the staff at the Library?'

He admitted that he had told the lawyer none of these things. The reason for holding back, he explained, was that he was a gentleman after all and could not be expected to say such things of a lady.

Without a word of it to Borges, a few days later I wrote a letter to the lawyer after his return to Córdoba. 'I want to say that in this private matter you have been seeing Borges about, I may ... be of help to you. I know things that perhaps Borges has not told you and that may be useful to you.' I asked him to phone me the next time he visited Buenos Aires.

Why was Borges covering up? Was it shame that he had allowed so much to transpire without taking action or seeking redress much sooner? Why at this critical moment had he exposed himself as so weak, bloodless, faint-hearted? Could it have been doña Leonor's telling explanation that 'Georgie has no backbone'?

Fernández Ordóñez returned to the city a few days later. He phoned and I suggested we have tea together. He chose a place he liked, the Molino, an old-fashioned *confitería*, or tea room, adjacent to the Congress.

'I know what you and Borges talked about the other day,' I said.

'You speak; I'm listening,' he said, the epitome of discretion.

I recited a litany of things about Elsa that Borges had not told him. When I finished I asked if there was enough here to warrant a divorce. Plenty, he said. But he also said that legally there would be more to the picture than what I had just planted.

To call a waiter's attention, I could not escape noticing, Fernández Ordóñez would repeatedly strike the side of his glass with a teaspoon. Heads would turn. His action may have been acceptable behaviour in Córdoba but in snobbish Buenos Aires it was infra dig and marked him out as a provincial. But one of the things I liked about this lawyer was the authority that he radiated. He was clear and decisive in thought and action. This could only prove a boon to Borges. His authority, which was almost intimidating, was enhanced and reinforced by his sheer size.

Shortly after our meeting at the Molino, he and I and Borges went to consult a friend of mine, a local lawyer. The first thing we learned was that if a divorce were to be pursued, Fernández Ordóñez would be required to work with a Buenos Aires lawyer. Between the two present legal minds a bleak, realistic picture was then outlined. There was no divorce as such under Argentine law, only a form of legal separation that everyone referred to as divorce and that was as effective as any divorce except that it did not allow for remarriage.

None of this was positive or encouraging. Borges did not need to be painted a dark picture; he was already living it.

Time drifted. Borges seemed to be dragging his feet. Suddenly Elsa, as if she sensed something afoot, was on her best behaviour. It now became painful to me to hear Borges excusing her. 'She's just a child,' he said. 'She can't get along without me.'

His creative mind was firmly fixed on his new set of stories. He was desperate to finish the book and was working on it at breakneck speed. Never before in his life had he written so much in so short a time. But I thought his rush was dangerous. Once he finished a story, of which I was its first reader, he refused to reconsider the slightest detail and was all nerves just to get to the end. Somehow

– but I could not figure why or how exactly – the book had become inextricable from his domestic problems.

One day he lamented that Silvina Bullrich had been mocking him for not publishing anything for years. I judged this to be untrue and merely another excuse for justifying whatever he had in mind to do. Silvina, with whom Borges had once been romantically attached, was a prolific novelist and story writer. She was also a beautiful, independent, outspoken woman. In gossipy Buenos Aires it was damningly said of her books that they were read by housemaids. Years later, immediately after General Galtieri had invaded the Falkland Islands, it was Silvina Bullrich – the only one of all the writers in the Argentine – who stuck her head above the parapet and published a vitriolic letter in *La Nación* condemning the war and the regime. Unlike so many of her fellow Argentines of that day, Silvina was wanting in neither courage nor conviction.

There was another problem with Borges's proposed volume of stories. He was touting it as a kind of Argentine *Plain Tales from the Hills*, one of his favourite Kipling books. For his collection Borges planned eight stories, forgetting the fact that Kipling's *Plain Tales* was a relatively encyclopedic compendium of forty stories. One trouble was, the way I saw it, that Borges kept chopping everything down to bare bones, to outlines, to plots. Once, in Cambridge, he had said to me, 'I want to write honestly but in advance I know I'll fall victim to certain literary temptations – to lump certain details and to pad others.' He was adamant in his impatience.

I feared that readers would consider a book of eight rather thin stories a feeble effort. I communicated my misgivings in a letter to Bioy Casares, who was on a long European tour visiting spas and having mud baths to cure a serious lumbago problem. Bioy agreed with me and sent back a letter to Borges that I was to read to him. The letter briefly urged his friend not to make his book too short. I read the letter to Borges but he did not want to hear what Bioy had to say.

Elsa now began a smear campaign against me, I suppose in a last ditch effort to turn Borges against me. She bandied it about that I was not only stealing Borges's time but I was stealing money from him as well. I mentioned this to Borges and asked him to do something about it. I knew deep down that he would not dare tell her to stop. Elsa was exercising some power or hold over him which had turned him into a sheep.

There was a further setback a couple of weeks later when Borges explained that he could not proceed on the divorce front until Bioy returned. Until such time he was just sitting tight. One more excuse, I thought. Meanwhile, more and more frequently, doña Leonor was inviting me to her flat in Calle Maipú, where she lost no time in blackening Elsa's name and urging me to get Georgie to take decisive action.

A month passed with no indication as to when Bioy would be coming back. Borges kept pressing me to get a date from him. I wrote and told Bioy that Georgie was getting more and more weary with his home life but now seemed prepared to act. 'If only Bioy were here,' I reported to Bioy that Borges kept saying to mc. 'I must wait until Bioy comes back. When will he be back?' I also told him that doña Leonor phoned me two or three times a week to find out if he had written to me with the date of his reappearance. 'She has all her hopes pinned on you because Borges has evidently mentioned that he is waiting for your return.'

I knew I was pushing it with Bioy but what other choice had I? I was pushing it with Fernández Ordóñez too. I wrote to inform him that Borges was fretting over two things. 'One, that you once told him that things could drag out for months or even years. If I may give the lawyer advice, I think this sort of negative prospect hurts rather than helps. I think it is best to tell B. that things can be worked out.' I'd felt obliged to calm Borges by saying that the lawyer had seemed negative because he did not know all the facts of the case nor the gravity of the situation. I was trying to convince Borges to open up. 'The other thing that worries Borges is his books,' I told Fernández Ordóñez. 'He is afraid that once he announces a plan, she may destroy them. I told him I was sure you could prevent that legally . . . It would be good if you could give Borges assurances on this point.'

A further word about Bioy may be called for. I have mentioned my ceaseless pressuring him for the date of his return. It should have been obvious to him that I was acting at Borges's behest as well as doña Leonor's, but apparently it wasn't. On his return Bioy vented his anger on me but he was not one hundred per cent truthful. He said he felt bad enough that Georgie needed him and that he could not respond. My hounding him had made things worse. What he failed to mention – and I only found out later – was that his European trip was an extended skirmish to rid himself of a woman who was pressing him to marry her.

Bioy was a wily don Juan. A decade or two later, a woman approached me at some gathering and said, 'So you're di Giovanni. I've hated you for twenty years.' 'But we've never met before,' I said. She then went on to tell me that instead of visiting her evenings, Bioy would claim he had to work with taskmaster di Giovanni. Bioy and I did work together some evenings, but not that many.

While all this was transpiring Fernández Ordóñez drafted a ten-page-long, didactic letter and sent it to me with a request to read it to Borges. The missive, for Borges's sake, was not without one or two literary touches. 'This letter is not for *gens de robe*,' the lawyer began, 'but for someone who confessed – without being believed – to a Ptolemaic ignorance in questions of Law.'

I am drafting these lines based on some notes I made in the past few days. I shall send them to you exactly as they leap from my fingers onto the keys of my typewriter. I foresee mistakes, poor style, and deletions, but I want to avoid any secretarial participation, which might lead to the possibility of indiscretion. I must tell you, therefore, that the subject of your marital discord is well known in Buenos Aires. Before I last saw you, a journalist friend who knows of my connection with you and your mother – he once accompanied me on a visit to doña Leonor – asked me about this. Of course, I said I had no knowledge of it.

The legal master then dissects for the innocent pupil the two components of Law – basic statutes and acts, and the interpretations and rulings of judges. He continues, explaining the two types of divorce in Argentine law – the first, which requires that grounds be specified in law (adultery, abandonment, excessive cruelty), with evidence provided; and the second, which, if it requires grounds, does not ask that they be specified or submitted in writing. This second type is based on the mutual consent of the spouses. Both types have in common, amongst other things, a main characteristic. They are divorces – here Fernández Ordóñez drops in a couple of terms of Roman law – *ad torum et mensam* and not *ad vinculum*. This means that divorce applies only to the living arrangements – the bed and the table – but that no matter how the divorce is obtained, neither spouse may marry again.

The lawyer goes on to say that from what Borges informed him, his case would fall into the category of *injurias graves* – excessive abuse. For this, to determine the excessiveness of the abuse, the judge takes into consideration a spouse's education, social position, etc. Fernández Ordóñez then lists various kinds of abuse, among which are:

language, behaviour, or deeds by one of the spouses that result in damage to the other;

any breach of the obligations of the marriage and any violation of either spouse's self-respect;

any damage, physical or moral, to our personality, whether caused by behaviour, language, or any other means.

It is not necessary for there to be *animus injuriandi* – that is, a specific intention to offend. Acts of misconduct committed with the knowledge that they might be an affront to the other spouse are enough ...

Even if the law employs the plural, several deeds or words are not necessary. One, sufficiently excessive, is enough.

The seriousness is determined by elements and circumstances appropriate to the individuals involved.

After a humorous reference to Job and a serious quote from a weighty legal tome (volume 83, page 284), the lawyer provides a list of examples of excessive abuse.

Among them, with passing references to Aristotle, Montaigne, Proust, Bernard Shaw and Mrs Campbell, are the following:

Abuse such as one spouse's not allowing the other to enter the matrimonial home.

Abusive correspondence not only between spouses but also involving third parties ...

Inconsiderateness: not inviting a wife to the ordination to the priesthood of her husband's brother; complete indifference: the woman who is not waiting for her husband when he comes home from military service.

Departures of the wife on travels without informing her husband of her destination or telling him beforehand.

The husband who frequently absents himself from the home for considerable lengths of time for no given reason.

The husband or wife keeping their marital status hidden to third parties.

Unfaithfulness that falls short of adultery: the husband going out with other women ...

The revelation that the other spouse is a communist does not constitute excessive abuse.

Failure to provide support, not only material but also moral: the husband who pays living expenses but does not visit his wife.

Artificial insemination using fluid not the husband's without the husband's approval.

Emotional attachment, even if chaste, of the husband to another woman . . .

Questions of inheritance: excessive meddling by the woman in the husband's personal affairs.

Homosexuality.

Failure to consummate the marital union.

The woman's having lied about her age by three years when she married. The incident was invoked by the husband twenty years later. His claim was dismissed.

Overbearing, wrought-up nature of the woman in contrast to the equanimity of the husband.

Silence of the husband, who went months without speaking

a word (I think he would have found the Trappist order more suitable than marriage).

At the bottom of page six of his letter, Fernández Ordóñez turns to Borges's case. He states that the specific instances mentioned to him by Borges constituted, in his opinion, *injurias graves* – excessive abuse. It will be necessary, he goes on, to consider the evidence. He then confides how much 'desk work' means to him, surrounded by papers, outlines, and even drawings, not to mention the benefits of concentration, of turning things over and over in the mind, of ruminating.

It is incredible how old memories suddenly emerge to provide evidence hitherto not taken into account; and, above all, how the mind is able to organize and muster all this in a strategic manner as if preparing for war ...

You told me that your wife had informed you of a transaction whereby money was taken from your joint funds to buy a property for her son. This, if done without your consent, unquestionably constitutes excessive abuse. The evidence will be irrefutable. Moreover, in my view the transaction is revocable.

A word or two on inheritance rules and regulations pertaining to marriage – but only what you need to know for now.

Clarifications and details can come later on; I am open to questions.

That which is held in common in a marriage is only what was acquired during the marriage ... Thus, your beloved books, which were yours before the marriage, belong to no one but you. (It's obvious that, when the time comes, you will have to prove that they were yours, but this will be easy and simple.) Also, any property that was yours before the marriage remains yours.

Books – and other property, personal or real estate – given to you after the marriage or obtained through inheritance or a legacy (in layman's language, the same thing) are also yours. Whatever books you acquired with money accrued during the marriage are, technically, joint property. There is a theory, however, with a certain basis in law and that seems to me applicable in your case, according to which personal property – books, for example – acquired after the marriage with joint assets but for the personal use of one spouse is the property of that spouse.

But even if this property – let us say books, because I know that this is your prime interest – was acquired after the marriage and with joint money and was therefore joint property, it would not be taken from you to become part of some unholy list for a public sale or dispersed amongst the impure hands of strangers. In the final settlement such intimate friends of yours – friends, more than objects – will remain in your possession. Tranquillity, then, for you and for the books in question.

You mentioned your wife's objection to your removing books from the house to take to the Library or wherever. You are the proprietor of your books – those you had before the marriage and those you bought after – and may take them wherever you please. The problem of dividing property, as to whether or not it was acquired during the marriage, can be resolved only when the partnership is dissolved, not before. Meanwhile, items can be used according to how it suits each spouse. There is no walled enclosure to keep some in and let others out. It's as if you were to insist that she cannot carry her lipstick in her handbag and has to put on her make-up at home and that the lipstick must remain in the bathroom medicine cabinet. Unless she thinks you are involved in a furtive separation. Which – apart from revealing an appalling ignorance of who you are – constitutes excessive abuse; indeed, most excessive.

In three paragraphs it is not possible, dear Borges, to sum up even in broad terms the rules governing property rights in a marriage; but – I insist – you must not complicate your life just now with such details . . .

In the first type of divorce – the one with grounds and evidence – culpability is important. The spouse found to be at fault has different rights from those of the injured party . . .

In the second type – that of mutual consent – the assets of the two parties are compared – with certain distinctions that for now I am going to omit. The assets of the spouse declared at fault in the first type of divorce are compared with those of the spouse who has consented to a divorce by mutual consent.

Unless she sees financial advantages in the first type of divorce, the second type – a divorce by mutual consent – avoiding scandal and great costs, would be the best choice for her.

If a divorce by mutual consent is granted:

the duties of cohabitation and spiritual maintenance cease (material maintenance remains in certain exceptional circumstances. Pardon me again; my duty is to explain to you everything that the Law states . . .)

neither spouse may remarry;

the duty of fidelity remains;

the marriage is dissolved; the property is divided;

maintenance: in the first type of divorce, the guilty spouse has rights to alimony only in the case of extreme necessity (I do not tire of begging your pardon: I am operating in theoretical territory and am trying to be exhaustive);

in the second type of divorce the same thing occurs; *it may be agreed that one of the spouses will give alimony to the other*, and the sum specified. This obligation may be revoked should the beneficiary commit some subseqent indiscretion, calumny, etc.;

inheritance rights: in the first type of divorce, *the guilty spouse inherits nothing from the innocent*; the innocent party does inherit from the guilty;

in the second type of divorce, *neither spouse inherits from the other*. (In certain cases exceptions may be made that we lawyers are able to arrange) . . .

Fernández Ordóñez closes the letter on a note of contriteness, confessing to have sinned in his wordiness. 'As someone said, I was in too much of a hurry to be brief . . .'

Plainly what he wrote was a labour of love and a matter of great pride to him. Alas, Borges could not find it in himself to appreciate this. I tried to read the whole document to him, but he was so distressed and distraught by the circumstances of his daily existence that he could not work up the patience to take in the lawyer's many points. All Georgie wanted to hear was the news that concerned his books.

For me, the fact that Elsa had bought a flat for her son was a revelation but not a surprise. Borges did not seem overly concerned about which of the two courses of divorce might befall him. He just wanted it over at any cost.

23   The Reckoning

It was a source of amazement to me, given his initial inability or reluctance to provide Fernández Ordóñez with even a shred of evidence that might serve as grounds for a divorce, the way when it came down to it Borges caught fire and threw himself headlong into the task. The lawyer had asked me to sit down with Georgie and, in light of what I had leaked to him, draw up a comprehensive list of Elsa's transgressions. 'Put down everything,' Fernández Ordóñez had instructed. 'I'll decide what is useful.'

Borges and I chose a Saturday morning for the job. The Library was closed on Saturdays and there would be no one – we were thinking of the secretaries – to interrupt us or to pry into what we were up to. I'd had to warn the lawyer not to phone Borges at the Biblioteca Nacional under any circumstances. We had found out that a new secretary, a Mrs De Ferrari, on loan from the library of the Congress – the Congress had been shut down by the military government – had been spying to find out what Borges was up to with me and Fernández Ordóñez. She told this to one of the other secretaries, who told me.

Mrs De Ferrari was nosy but she was also cheerful, and a tireless worker. She eagerly took down Borges's dictation for his new stories. Borges liked the fact that she was completely uncritical and never annoyed him by venturing a suggestion. In fact, she was like a machine. If somewhere in a sentence Borges dictated the word semicolon, we later found the word 'semicolon', and not the symbol for it, in the typescript. This amused Borges no end.

On that Saturday we sat at the big table in his office, and I pulled the large typewriter into place before me. Adjusting a sheet of paper into the roller, I then typed the number one and waited.

Borges was not forthcoming. 'Remember that time in Cambridge when . . .' I said, trying to prime him.

It brought no response. 'Remember what she did that night at the Rockefellers'?'

'Just a moment,' Borges said, and he slipped out for an Old Norse.

He came back another man, one with an appetite.

'Put this down,' he said. And so we got started. Here is the list as we wrote, rewrote, and corrected it:

1. For the past three years I have been unable to step inside my home without fear of recrimination, brooding silences, and

all kinds of moodiness. My wife demands an explanation and justification for my every word or action.

2. She is hostile to my family and to almost all my friends. To avoid disagreeable scenes I cannot invite any of them home.

3. She interferes in my private business, and has tried to get my secretaries at the National Library to report on my correspondence, my telephone conversations, and my visitors.

4. On several occasions she has spoken to José Edmundo Clemente, my deputy at the National Library, about [her] becoming personally involved in the running of this institution.

5. She has interfered with and tried to destroy my relationship with Norman Thomas di Giovanni, with whom I am collaborating on the translation into English of eleven of my books for the New York publisher E. P. Dutton.

6. She has not shown the slightest interest in my literary work but only in the financial rewards of that work.

7. When I am asked to deliver lectures, she criticizes me if I do not demand exorbitant fees, and she becomes furious when I give free talks to libraries, schools, or groups of students.

8. She tries to force mediocre company on me, and she

distrusts *a priori* all writers, whom she refers to as 'a pack of dogs'.

9. She has attempted to break off my old friendship with Néstor Ibarra, who has translated so much of my work with admirable intelligence and great affection. She has insulted him in a rude and unseemly manner.

10. She despises my family and loses no opportunity to tell me so.

11. It annoys her that I partially maintain my mother, who has just turned ninety-four. Elsa keeps pestering me to tell her exactly how much I give my mother and has even asked employees of my publishers, Editorial Emecé, to reveal the amount to her.

12. She has tried to get my friends to tell her how much I spend each day. When she visited Europe I never asked her how much money she spent. Nor on our trips to the United States did I ever ask what she spent money on.

13. In these past three years she has never admitted once to being wrong about anything. I cannot recall having heard from her lips a single word of kindness or generosity. She complains about everything and everyone.

14. She is always telling the most astonishing lies about someone or other.

15. She knows that I am almost completely blind and she brags about helping me as little as possible. During our stay in Cambridge (September 1967-April 1968), I received two unfriendly letters, which she insisted on keeping and rereading to me as proof that many people hate me.

16. When she is annoyed with me she threatens to expose me. She often tells strangers in front of me that I am hard to get along with and not the person they think I am. She told a friend of mine that she wanted to destroy the favourable image the other person held of me.

17. I know she has said she does not love me but only puts up with me for financial reasons.

18. On the day of our civil marriage my mother told Elsa that to her only a church ceremony counted. Elsa said that if I died that night she would inherit half my assets. The term 'marital possessions' exerts a strange spell over her.

19. During our stay in Cambridge her behaviour forced me to leave her and to spend several nights in a hotel. More than once she told me that I was insufferable and that she was going to leave me; I told her the door was open. In Cambridge

she managed to alienate almost all my University colleagues, alleging imaginary grievances. She did not want us to attend a gathering of professors because I was not the guest of honour and this is what she told those who had invited us.

20. She did not want me to pay Margarita Guerrero, my collaborator in *The Book of Imaginary Beings*, the amount due to her for the translation of the book into English. Elsa claims that all those who have collaborated with me have been mere secretaries.

21. In Cambridge she unsuccessfully tried to persuade my secretary John Murchison to get me to demand much higher fees for my lectures than I had been offered. Once, after taking the money for one of my lectures, she angered me by asking for a larger fee.

22. In Oklahoma (November 1969) she claimed that the fee the university had paid me was utterly ridiculous but she did not want to turn it down. This occurred more than once. In the United States she would refuse invitations and claim that I had refused them because she was afraid (she told me this) that everyone would speak English and use that language to make fun of her.

23. The Rockefellers invited us to dinner at their home. Elsa took advantage of the occasion to whip out a camera

and take pictures of the various rooms, not even sparing the bathroom. The object of this strange manoeuvre was to impress her family and women friends with these elegant images. She asked Rockefeller himself to help her get through customs items destined for charitable causes. These were items she had bought for herself.

24. She wants me to replace my friends, who share my literary tastes, with others of a more commercial persuasion.

25. She is troubled for some obscure jealous reason by my current and past friends, my family, and even my ancestors.

26. I found myself forced to turn down a doctorate *honoris causa* from Oxford University so as to avoid the unpleasantness of a trip with her (June 1969). Elsa approved of my decision when she learned that the University was not going to pay our expenses.

27. In the past year, when my mother underwent an operation, the first thing Elsa said was that my sister and I should share equally the costs of the funeral. She constantly advises my mother to find cheaper doctors and even offered to do this for her.

I posted this list to Fernández Ordóñez, ignorant of its potential import or of what use would be made of it. In a covering letter I told him that Borges was now anxious for action; each day was an agony for him. He had given up waiting for Bioy's return.

In fact, for Borges the gloves were off; our list was a long overdue declaration of war.

24   Amongst the Lawyers

How Borges and I got any of our literary work done in the weeks that followed is a mystery to me. And yet we did. He finished writing the eleven tales of *El informe de Brodie* and immediately, towards the middle of April 1970, I began to read the stories back to him so that we could give them their final shape and decide on their order for the book.

Borges had firm ideas about how to place his stories in a volume. You put a few of your best, or strongest, stories at the beginning; you buried the weaker ones in the middle; and you closed the book with more of the finest work. He always placed a title story last. In this way, he reasoned, you hooked the reader at the outset, let him doze a bit in the middle, and then woke him up with a bang at the end. There might be one other element. Stories with similar themes would be presented back to back. I found the whole scheme incontrovertible. With *Brodie* we had two cracks at this. For our translated edition, called *Doctor Brodie's Report*, we adopted a variant pattern that we thought more suited to the English-speaking reader.

The final reading and ordering of *Brodie* was a week's work, five days, Monday to Friday. The following Monday Borges wrote the collection's foreword and we delivered the completed typescript to his publisher. On the very next day we began to write directly in English his autobiography. This enterprise, entered into with the high hopes of composing about thirty pages in two weeks' time, turned into an unspeakable ordeal. In the first three working sessions we drafted sixteen pages. Then, with the pressure of other more immediate duties and an endless stream of interrupting visitors, a week passed before we could complete another page and a half. The autobiographical piece, as I have mentioned, was my dreamchild, and there was a stringent deadline for its completion. I knew pressures would only grow worse when the meetings with his team of lawyers eventually took place. And then, to be squeezed in, there were the pages of Mrs Stone's promised introduction. I was in utter despair.

And on the divorce front? Things were creeping along, invisibly but inexorably. Borges had thrown himself headlong into work as an antidote to his grinding personal troubles.

The day after we drew up his list of grievances against Elsa was a Sunday. We repaired to the Library again, this time to correct the proofsheets of his *Brodie* stories. This gave Borges a legitimate pretext for an extra outing away from the Belgrano flat. It took us three days in all to complete the job; I then spent a fourth reading through the proofs on my own before delivering the book to Emecé. At this same time Borges completed a draft of the longest story he ever wrote – 'El Congreso'.

On three of the next four Saturdays we managed once more to evade Belgrano and to work at the Library. Our labours were legitimate. There was the autobiography, hopelessly limping along, yet to my great relief we tackled and finished the Grolier piece for Mrs Stone. That took five working sessions over four days.

We wove into this crowded schedule a first meeting with the Buenos Aires lawyer, Eduardo Martínez Carranza. The participants were Borges, Fernández Ordóñez, me, and Martínez's son, who was just starting out on a legal career. Martínez Carranza's offices were on the twelfth floor of an elegant building on Leandro Alem opposite the Casa Rosada and within sight of the monumental Central Post Office. This was an easy walk for Borges and me from the National Library.

The offices were just what you expected of a successful Buenos Aires law firm. The reddish mahogany conference table gleamed to a high polish. The impressive wall of bookshelves contained perfectly ordered rows of legal tomes. There was not a stray sheet of paper to be seen anywhere. The place was immaculate and impeccable.

What was expected of me in this picture I had no idea. I thought I was simply accompanying Borges on my arm from Calle México to Leandro Alem. The lawyers thought otherwise. Our first session was more or less for the purposes of orientation. The legal team spoke their jargon and broadly outlined plans and subsequent procedure. They were going to need a great deal of information about Borges's financial affairs that he could not provide them with but that I could. I was also put in charge of delivering some advance money to cover the lawyers' initial fees. We were going to be meeting there again for several days running during the next week.

Borges was not about to go to his bank and withdraw a large sum from funds he held jointly with Elsa. But he had his secret weapon – the uncollected accumulation over years of the royalties on his many books published by Emecé. I never quite understood the arrangement. I had accompanied Borges on numerous occasions out to the publisher's headquarters at Alsina 2049, twenty or so blocks from the Library. These errands were not only to turn in typescripts and pick up contracts but also to collect the small sums Borges liked to have for pocket money or for assisting his mother. These were the sums, in banknotes, that Borges hid at home between the pages of the *Britannica* and that Elsa knew all about.

I now took a taxi alone out to Alsina, where I was to collect the rather large amount of money the lawyers had requested. Borges had phoned ahead to tell Emecé to give me whatever I asked for. When I arrived and stated specifically what I wanted, I – or my demand – was met with disbelief.

'We don't keep that kind of money on hand.'

I noted an angry tone in their reply, which made me say, 'But it's Borges's money and we need it urgently.'

There was grumbling and fretting.

'We'll have to go to the bank for such a sum,' I was told. 'You'll have to come back.'

So the publisher was sitting on Borges's money, in their account, and I doubt he was ever paid any interest. Alas, the arrangement suited him.

A few days later I went back and picked up the money. The roll of bills was so thick that my trouser pocket bulged obscenely. I could hardly wait to get safely back to Leandro Alem, where I could rid myself of it. I had been paid in Argentine moneda nacional; the equivalent in dollars of this instalment was something like $8,500.

From here on the meetings were in the nature of war games. We all sat around the table and, playing devil's advocate, the lawyers took Elsa's side, presenting the case from her point of view. They were asking themselves what if she contested the evidence against her, what if she refused to seek a divorce by mutual consent. No one knew when the time came what her lawyers might advise her.

Fernández Ordóñez and Martínez Carranza also began a first look into Georgie and Elsa's assets. I was assigned to meet Luis de Torre, a lawyer and one of Borges's nephews.

Luis prepared his uncle's taxes and had at his fingertips the amounts of Borges's university pension, his Library stipend, his earnings from Emecé, and so forth.

The rudiments of a picture were beginning to emerge. From Borges a burden had been lifted. He was now paying professionals to deal with his problems. Other concerned parties were also coming to his aid. One was the young, ambitious film-maker Hugo Santiago, who for months had been working with Bioy and Borges on the script of a feature called *Invasión*. I knew too much about Borges's essays into script writing ever to become enthusiastic about Hugo's film. Much of my feeling was subjective. The film was in black-and-white and many scenes had been shot at night. For me this was just too depressing as Buenos Aires was then at the mercy of a black-and-white dictatorship and everything seemed tainted with a touch of sinister darkness. It never failed to impress me whenever I returned to Argentina from abroad just how gloomy the city was at night. Even the billboards along the 9 de Julio – Argentines claimed it was the widest avenue in the world – seemed dingy and underlit. It was no wonder that *porteños* with money, whenever they could, flocked to New York, London, and Paris.

As for Borges the screenwriter, he collaborated with Bioy and published in 1951 a volume of two scripts, *Los orilleros* and *El paraíso de los creyentes*. Alas, a look into the book tells you that Borges had read too much Bernard

Shaw. The speeches are too long; the films depend too heavily on the spoken word. There was one speech at the culmination of *Invasión* when the protagonist seemed to have stepped onto a soapbox and held forth on courage and action. One has only to look into Borges's short stories to find similar examples of artificial and stilted dialogue. Fortunately, verbal exchanges between his characters are few and far between.

Borges's work with Hugo Santiago brought me into close contact with him. We became friends, we socialized, and I went to parties with the crème de la crème of Buenos Aires's Frenchified bohemians. These parties took place in rambling flats. In one room the talk was about 'happenings', in another the topic of discussion might be Claude Lévi-Strauss versus Jean-Paul Sartre, in a third a couple of silent young men were studiously bent over a chessboard. Hugo had a slender moustache that he constantly played with, one hand twirling the ends. This was not so much a nervous habit as it was his signature. He also wore a camel hair coat draped over his shoulders with studied nonchalance.

When the time came, Hugo became a generous key conspirator in the plot to free Borges.

25   The Night of the Oxford Martyrs

The lawyers had prepared the divorce papers for Borges to sign, and that brought to an end the opening phase of our dealings with them. There now remained some tricky practical issues. How were we going to extricate Borges from the Belgrano flat? How were we going to extricate his beloved books?

Borges knew that his only option was to leave town. He knew that he would have been unable to resist Elsa's pleas should he remain in Buenos Aires and she track him down. Unknown to me Borges had broached plans for an escape some months earlier and had kept these plans to himself and to Bioy.

Bioy went abroad at the beginning of February. Before he left Borges had asked him whether he should leave Elsa. He also asked, if necessary, whether he could hole up at Bioy's estancia for some days or possibly weeks. Of course Bioy consented. He gave Borges written instructions how to get to Rincón Viejo, near Pardo, on Route 3 a couple of hundred kilometres to the south of Buenos Aires. Borges promptly lost them, and months later I had to reiterate the plan to Bioy, asking again for permission, and telling him that I would probably be accompanying Borges. Bioy sent me a new set of instructions.

Like good conspirators we allowed no one knowledge of our whole plan. Fernández Ordóñez had booked us into a hotel in Córdoba that only Borges and I knew the name of. Borges's mother, now ninety-four, was punctilious in her rectitude. She feared that Elsa would be quick to ring for information, and while Leonor wanted to be able to say in truth that she did not know her son's whereabouts, she was nonetheless anxious to be able to reach him if need be. I gave her a telephone number on a slip of paper in a sealed envelope and had her watch me secrete it in a drawer of her desk. Our plans were laid and all that remained was to get through the next several days.

Our working sessions at the Library became perfunctory affairs. I had expected no less. Borges was in a pitiable funk, and I could not hope for his concentration. All I could do was to watch him, keep a careful eye on him, hold him from flagging in his resolve. He was silent, he drifted, and it was impossible to lift his spirits. It is no exaggeration to say that the days dragged without end.

It was close to eight o'clock on the night of 6 July 1970. Borges and I trudged slowly home from the Library. For some reason, or for no reason, we chose to walk up Mexico Street or was it Venezuela. For three or four blocks along the route the houses were boarded up for demolition, part of the works for the extension of the broad 9 de Julio. Dust lay thickly on all the doorsteps and on the spiny leaves of the bruised agaves in the front gardens. The night was foggy and chill, gloomy, and not a soul roamed the streets. From the sky sifted down the kind of mist that the Argentines call *garúa*. This mist is so fine that it is not considered precipitation. We plodded home, a weight on him, a weight on me, because I was not sure he could do it and I don't think he was either. He clung to my arm but neither of us spoke a word. We were dreading the moment when we would reach his door.

The struggle to establish a Protestant Church in England was slow and bloody. When Henry VIII died, in 1547, his three heirs were his son Edward and his two daughters, Mary and Elizabeth. Edward VI, known as 'the Boy King', reigned only until 1553. With his strong Protestant advisors, he had the Latin church services translated into English. Upon his death, the throne passed to his sister Mary, a determined Roman Catholic. She believed that the best way to deal with heresy – that is, Protestantism – was to burn as many heretics as possible. It was during her reign that the three Oxford martyrs were committed to the funeral pyre. During Mary's Counter-Reformation it is said that nearly three hundred Protestants were convicted of heresy and condemned to death.

Hugh Latimer and Nicholas Ridley were two of her victims. Latimer was appointed Bishop of Worcester in 1535 but was forced to resign the post when he fell into conflict with Henry VIII. Ridley held a number of church posts, serving as one of the King's Chaplains in 1540-41; he was also made Master of Pembroke College. He managed to escape punishment on a charge of heresy in 1543 and became Bishop of Rochester in 1547 and then Bishop of London in 1550. He had helped Archbishop Thomas Cranmer with the Book of Common Prayer in 1548. The basic tenets of the Protestants were two. One, that church services be conducted in English; and two, that the intercession of a priest beween man and God was unnecessary.

The following vivid account of the burnings of Hugh Latimer and Nicholas Ridley appears in John Foxe's *Book of Martyrs*:

> Dr. Ridley, the night before execution, was very facetious, had himself shaved, and called his supper a marriage feast; he remarked upon seeing Mrs. Irish (the keeper's wife) weep, 'though my breakfast will be somewhat sharp, my supper will be more pleasant and sweet.'
>
> The place of death was on the north side of the town opposite Baliol College: – Dr. Ridley was dressed in a black gown furred, and Mr. Latimer had a long shroud on, hanging down to his feet. Dr. Ridley, as he passed Bocardo [Prison], looked up to see Dr. Cranmer, but the latter was then engaged in a disputation with

a friar. – When they came to the stake, Dr. Ridley embraced Latimer fervently, and bid him be of good heart. He then knelt by the stake, and after earnestly praying together, they had a short private conversation. Dr. Smith then preached a short sermon against the martyrs, who would have answered him, but were prevented by Dr. Marshal, the vice-chancellor. Dr. Ridley then took off his gown and tippet, and gave them to his brother-in-law, Mr. Shipside. He gave away also many trifles to his weeping friends, and the populace were anxious to get even a fragment of his garments. Mr. Latimer gave nothing, and from the poverty of his garb, was soon stripped to his shroud, and stood venerable and erect, fearless of death.

Dr. Ridley being unclothed to his shirt, the smith placed an iron chain about their waists and Dr. Ridley bid him fasten it securely; his brother having tied a bag of gunpowder about his neck, gave some also to Mr. Latimer. Dr. Ridley then requested of Lord Williams, of Fame, to advocate with the queen the cause of some poor men to whom he had, when bishop, granted leases, but which the present bishop refused to confirm. A lighted fagot was now laid at Dr. Ridley's feet, which caused Mr. Latimer to say, 'Be of good cheer, Ridley; and play the man. We shall this day, by God's grace, light up such a candle in England, as, I trust, will never be put out.' When Dr. Ridley saw the flame approaching him, he exclaimed, 'Into thy hands, O Lord, I commend my spirit!' and repeated often, 'Lord receive my spirit!' Mr. Latimer, too, ceased not to say, 'O Father of heaven receive my soul!' Embracing the flame, he bathed his hands in it, and soon died, apparently, with little pain; but Dr. Ridley, by the ill-adjustment of the fagots, which were green, and placed too high above the furze was burnt much downwards. At this time, piteously, entreating for more fire to come to him, his brother-in-law imprudently heaped the fagots up over him, which caused the fire more fiercely to burn his limbs, whence he literally leaped up and down under the fagots, exclaiming that he could not burn; indeed, his dreadful extremity was but too plain, for after his legs were quite consumed, he showed his body and shirt unsinged by the flame. Crying upon God for mercy, a man with a bill pulled the fagots down, and when the flames arose, he bent himself towards that side; at length the gunpowder was ignited, and then he ceased to move, burning on the other side, and falling down at Mr. Latimer's feet over the chain that had hitherto supported him.

Every eye shed tears at the afflicting sight of these sufferers, who were among the most distinguished persons of their time in dignity, piety, and public estimation. They suffered 16 October 1555.

The execution of the third Oxford Martyr, Thomas Cranmer, took place on the same spot opposite Baliol College some five months later, on 21 March 1556. Cranmer had been Archbishop of Canterbury in the reign of Henry VIII. Known as a brilliant translator, under Edward he promoted the worship of the Church in English and secured the use of new forms of liturgy. When Mary became queen she ordered him to return to the Roman obedience. Cranmer five times wrote a letter of submission to the Pope and to Roman Catholic doctrines and four times tore it up. Mary believed his last submission to be insincere, and Cranmer was ordered to be burned.

He was to repudiate his final letter and announce that he died a Protestant. 'I have sinned,' he said, 'in that I signed with my hand what I did not believe with my heart. When the flames are lit, this hand shall be the first to burn.' And so it was. When the flame licked closer, Cranmer held his right hand in the fire until it was burnt to a cinder. He did not speak or move, except once, when he raised his left hand to wipe the sweat from his brow.

The bailiffs of the City of Oxford petitioned the Archbishop of Canterbury for payment of the expenses incurred in dealing with the three martyrs. Cranmer's expenses included the cost of wine, figs, oysters, veal, and almonds as well as his barber and laundry charges. The last items to be listed were the hundred wood faggots and fifty furze faggots that formed his living pyre.

And the night of 6 July 1970? When Borges and I got to his doorstep, he turned to me and, paraphrasing – or perhaps not quite remembering – Bishop Latimer's words, said, 'We shall this day light a fire such as England never saw . . .'

A kind of short nervous laugh followed his words. Not even in such a dire moment could Borges resist an opportunity to air his learning and to savour a literary turn of phrase. This last night under the same roof with Elsa – was it going to prove his funeral pyre?

He opened the street door and stepped inside.

26   Escape to Córdoba

The morning, like the night before, was chill and grey. I was waiting, huddled in the doorway of the National Library, my neck craning for a glimpse of an approaching taxi. Was he going to show up? Was he going to go through with it?

A car drove up, a taxi, and its door was opening. I leapt out into the street and threw myself inside before Borges could emerge. And off we sped for the intown airport. Borges was a trembling leaf and utterly exhausted after a sleepless night. He confessed to me that his greatest fear had been that he might blurt the whole thing out to Elsa at any moment.

At the airport Hugo Santiago and my wife were waiting for us at the flight counter with a pair of single tickets to Córdoba. But we were to be foiled. The wintry weather was against us, and the fog delayed our flight. Borges, jittery and near collapse, thought the game was up. He saw Elsa materializing out of the mist and laying a hand on his shoulder. Santiago and I did our best to put Borges at ease, laughing at our own feeble attempts at gallows humour, but it was nervous laughter and both of us, I know, were quaking inside. Eventually, by twelve o'clock, our plane took off.

That was half the plan in motion. While we were sweating it out at the airport Fernández Ordóñez was knocking at the door of the Belgrano flat with a sheaf of legal documents in hand. He was accompanied by a couple of removal men with big wicker baskets ready to pack and spirit away Borges's books.

Fernández Ordóñez had arranged a room for us at the Hotel Astoria. The hotel was old-fashioned, and for some unknown reason the lawyer put us together in the same room. It contained a single bed and a big double bed. The arrangement was much to Borges's displeasure.

But we had more immediate problems to deal with. Borges had run away with no clothes. Out on the streets of Córdoba we found a men's shop, where we outfitted him with a pair of pyjamas, a new suit, underwear, etc. We decided Borges would wear the new dark-blue pin-stripe suit we had just bought him. After a minute the clerk returned with the trousers of the grey tweed suit Borges had been wearing. It was the same suit he had had the accident in. The clerk asked me what we wanted to do with it. Before I could tell him to make a package of it that we could take away, without a word that might have been embarrassing he held the trousers up and wiggled a finger through a hole in the seat. The hole was the size of a fifty-pence piece.

I told the clerk to dispose of them. My mind was trying to grapple with the fact that Elsa sent the man off to work at the Library every day with his clothes in this condition. But then I remembered how she once bragged to me that she used to buy Borges second-hand shoes.

All that afternoon Borges was utterly distraught. He clung to my arm more tightly than ever before, and at some point, as we stepped up onto a kerb, he simply slipped down, collapsing. I'd had to snatch at him before he went face down onto the pavement.

Fernández Ordóñez flew back to Córdoba, anxious to see us as soon as possible to report on the morning's events at the Belgrano flat. It seems that Olga was there with Elsa when he and the removal men arrived. It had all gone well; the books were safely retrieved, and Elsa appeared not to have been overly surprised by the lawyer's intrusion.

When Olga was leaving the flat, Fernández Ordóñez was eager to report – with him looking on not two steps away – the cousins gave each other a prolonged kiss on the lips. The lawyer was so struck by the unusualness of this that he repeated it to us several times. And then I remembered the incident in the Cambridge flat when I had suddenly startled Olga and Elsa, who had sprung up from under a blanket on the day-bed and Elsa had told me not to mention to Borges what I had seen.

Borges's only reaction was to say meekly – and he said it two or three times – that under the circumstances, by which he no doubt meant his impotence, he would have understood and not minded if Elsa had had a lover.

To Borges's great comfort and relief we moved the next day to the Windsor Hotel, where he had a room of his own. He had slept badly and was worn out, yet he insisted that he was all right and to prove it he gave a lecture on Leopoldo Lugones at the Hospital Privado. This was a mistake. He was utterly depleted and had no idea how to rest.

My wife had joined us, but we were not to make our getaway from Córdoba without first partaking of a banquet prepared for us by Fernández Ordóñez's wife. Abundance was in every dish. The meal ended with a monumental dessert that dripped honey.

We stayed two nights at the Windsor and the next day caught a plane back to Buenos Aires. Borges was satisfied that the lawyer had done his job. There was still much to be resolved on the legal front but for now the major ordeal was behind him. All Borges had to do was to stay away from the city for about another five or six days and to begin to recover the life he had lost some thirty-three months earlier.

The week turned out to be draining. I don't know whose idea it was that Borges should be delivering another lecture far to the south of the Province of Buenos Aires. Hugo Santiago collected us at the airport in a pickup truck, Heather included, and all day he drove us across the pampa to the town of Coronel Pringles. This was a good five hundred kilometre journey and was more than twice the distance to Bioy's estancia, where Borges and I would be hiding out. Why Coronel Pringles? Who had set this up? One of Borges's secretaries at the Library, Haydée Santillán, hailed from Pringles and in fact happened to be visiting her family when we arrived. Borges had chosen to lecture on events that took place in this part of the country – the nineteenth-century Indian raids and what Argentines call 'the conquest of the desert', by which is meant the extermination of the native population. Our little caravan reached the lecture hall only a minute or two before the talk was to begin. The place was packed and the audience was eager. But Borges was not at all well; worse, he would not recognize that he was not well.

It was obvious that his male pride was involved. No one was going to tell him what he could or could not do. He put on a brave face, stubbornly insisting that he was fit to travel these enormous distances, fit to engage in public speaking. He was proving to himself that the Elsa business was over and that as far as he was concerned life was back to normal. The reality was that he was on the edge of nervous collapse.

The public in Coronel Pringles loved him. They listened, but on such occasions I could never determine whether they understood what his lectures were about. It was the mere Borges presence that bewitched them, and they had come really to see him in the flesh, this figure, this hero of Argentine literature.

The next morning we set off for the town of Coronel Suárez, some seventy-five kilometres away. The town was named after Borges's great-grandfather, a cavalry hero in the South American wars of independence. We drove in a caravan, accompanied by the mayor of Pringles and other municipal officials. Halfway along the route we were greeted by their Suárez counterparts, who had sallied forth to welcome us.

Borges's spirits picked up when he could show us the monument to his great-grandfather, beneath which we were all duly photographed. The mayor, whose name was Lo Vecchio, escorted us around the town hall. Then a splendid midday banquet was laid on for us all.

We left in Hugo's pickup at three in the afternoon and did not arrive at Bioy's estancia until after dark. Bioy had written to me with elaborate instructions how to reach Rincón Viejo – but from Buenos Aires. He had even suggested we phone his steward, Oscar Pardo, and have him come to the city and collect us in his pickup truck. Now all that was unnecessary. The estancia was so remote that to have phoned Oscar Pardo in advance would have been a job. One had to ask an operator for long distance and then ask for a certain Señor Lámaro, 'the proprietor of the shop that contained the public telephone pompously titled public office', wrote Bioy, and then leave a message for Oscar Pardo to phone back at such an hour on such a day at such-and-such a telephone number.

Hugo and Heather left after lunch the next day, allowing Borges and me to get back to his autobiography. Rincón Viejo was cold, chill, dank. But Bioy's steward laid on crackling eucalyptus fires for us and by keeping close to the flames we managed to avoid frostbite.

It turned out a coincidence that at Pardo we reached the point in the story of Borges's life when he first met Bioy back in the 1930s. We got in a welcome two or three days' work.

It was now time to face returning to Buenos Aires.

27   The Mosquito and the Judge

We left Bioy's estancia at five in the morning and were back in Buenos Aires by ten. I delivered Borges to his mother's flat in Calle Maipú, where he had been living before his marriage. We later met at the Library for a conference with Fernández Ordóñez.

First we had a look into the room next to Borges's office to examine the storage of his books. Removed from the wicker baskets they arrived in, they had been stacked in columns along one wall. They looked dead, lifeless, almost as if they had just been dumped. The stacks seemed rather high to me and in danger of collapsing, but their storage here was meant to be but a temporary affair. Borges was silent and appeared bewildered. Was this disarray of his books driving home to him the collapse of his marriage?

Our first task with the lawyer was to retrieve from the Belgrano flat the rest of Borges's possessions. Some of these had been taken away on the morning of our escape. I had torn a lined leaf out of a notebook of mine, and Borges and I had drawn up the following list:

2 elec. shavers

total contents of his bedroom

books living room and bedroom

globe

3 pictures by Xul-Solar (2) & Dürer (1)

personal correspondence

personal papers (passport, etc.)

his bed

all portable bookshelves

clothes

his mail

medals

mss. cuadernos [manuscript notebooks]

There was another list too:

National Library ID to buy medicine at a discount

2 Roman engravings

shovel from Casilda

2 Baccarat jugs

blue tray with Saxon warriors

set of records of Beowulf

Larousse dictionary

photographs (in Library)

contracts in her possession

medallion

In these first days back in Buenos Aires Borges faced a melancholy, humiliating task. He wanted to check the balance of his joint account with Elsa. I accompanied him to the bank and stood directly behind him at the counter, my ear cocked over his shoulder as he spoke to the clerk.

'I want to know how much money is in my account,' Borges said.

The clerk shuffled through some records and told Borges he no longer had an account at the bank.

'There must be some mistake,' Borges said.

'I'm sorry,' said the clerk, 'but you have no account with us.'

And then, exactly as had happened in Córdoba, Borges went limp and began to slip to the floor. I put my arms round him and pressed him against the counter to keep him upright.

The bank clerk seemed to want to be done with him.

I pulled Borges away from the window and began to trudge home with him. He was completely beside himself and kept repeating, 'There has to be some mistake.'

He phoned the bank from his flat and had the clerk's message confirmed. The bank had no money in any account under his name. He simply could not believe that Elsa had cleaned him out.

We found out later that when Borges and I left the bank, the clerk had phoned Elsa to say that Borges had been there

asking about his account. It seemed that Elsa had charmed
the man into doing her bidding. As I have mentioned, she
knew how to be chummy with certain people, and in this
case the clerk had been flattered into collusion.

We had no idea what had happened to the money, where
she had hidden it. We knew exactly how much it was – the
equivalent in moneda nacional of about $10,000 – so I
suggested to the lawyer that when the time came for
totting up who got what in the divorce settlement this sum
simply be deducted from what Borges would have to pay
Elsa. That was what happened, and Elsa made no objection.
Still, she lost no opportunity to taunt Borges that he and
I had not been able to trace the missing money. What in
fact she had done was simply to open a new account in
the same bank, in her name alone, and to place the money
there. Something like Poe's purloined letter, the solution
was under our noses all the time.

We were threading our way through the trail of Elsa's
treachery and still had the last chapter of the autobiography to complete, when one of those ubiquitous invitations
to deliver a lecture arrived. This talk was to take place far
to the south of the province in the town of Tres Arroyos.
For his subject Borges chose the poet Almafuerte. All the
arrangements had been made for us – air travel, hotel, etc.
So, just three weeks after the Córdoba escapade, we found
ourselves on the road again.

At the intown airport I inquired for the desk of the

airline we were to fly on. I was told to go to the Portuguese
National Airlines, where we would be directed. There we
were ushered past the desk straight out onto the airfield to
the foot of our plane. One look at our carrier and I literally fell to the tarmac in an uncontrollable fit of laughter.
I had never before seen such a tiny aircraft. We were not
travelling on an aeroplane, I told Borges; we were travelling on a mosquito.

We flew at about 2,000 feet, which gave us a stunning
view of the green pampa below. The plane seated seven and
was not full. A couple of canvas mail sacks were thrown in
behind us. I sat on the aisle and Borges by the window. We
had been aloft nearly an hour when Borges began acting
strangely. His hands roamed over the glass of the window,
circling and circling, and it was plain that he was in some
kind of distress.

'Where's the stewardess?' he asked after a while.

'There is no stewardess,' I told him.

'Well, I badly need an Old Norse,' he announced.

At the front of the plane was a small door behind which
was the pilot, whom we never laid eyes on. At the back
were the mail sacks. I got up and kneeled by one of them,
trying to tear it open. I was going to dump out its contents
and let Borges piss into it. But struggle as I might, I could
not break the seal. I returned to my seat, foreseeing what
was about to happen. We were still a long way from our
destination.

Then suddenly I noticed sticking out from a pocket of one of the empty seats ahead of us a plastic bag for air sickness. I grabbed it and held it open for Borges to use. When he finished there I was, sitting with a big warm bag of piss in my hands.

All at once without notice the plane swooped down and landed. A ladder was put up and the door was opened. I was the first one to reach it. I flung the bag out onto the tarmac and with great relief watched it explode. Though the stopover was only of a few minutes' duration Borges insisted we get out and use the loo 'just in case'.

We each had a room in the modern Parque Hotel. My room had two single beds. Borges lay stretched out on one and I sat on the edge of the other, a cleared bedside table between us as my desk. There we began to revise our draft of the closing pages of the autobiography. We were polishing not the fine words that come at the end of the finished work but emendations and additions to the conclusion of the previous paragraph, in which Borges speaks of longing to write under a pen name a merciless tirade against himself. 'Ah, the unvarnished truths I harbour!' he said.

Borges's talk went off well. Our hostess was an attractive woman, the local doctor's wife. After I had seen Borges off to bed, she and I went out and danced at a disco. The next afternoon Borges and I boarded the mosquito again for the flight back to Buenos Aires. The doctor's wife kindly drove us to the airfield and saw us off. He and I sat in the very same seats as before. This time the plane was full.

We were up in the air, and I soon dozed off. At some point I was wakened by an incredibly loud banging noise. I thought the plane was breaking up. Not far behind me, to my left, the plane's door had opened, and each time it swung out, the air current blew it back into position with an ear-shattering clatter. Another passenger, a youngish man, started for the racket in an attempt to shut the door firmly.

'No,' I told him, 'you might get sucked out!'

As he inched his way towards the door, I sat kneeling in my seat, wedged in, and reached out to hold him round the waist. It was no good. He could not get the latch to hold. But ingeniously he and I worked it out that if we used the plane's short aluminium ladder we could bridge the door opening and hook the ladder over its upright handle. It worked.

'What was going on?' Borges asked me.

I told him.

'Well,' he said, 'I was wondering what you were up to with your arms around that man's bum.'

I no sooner returned home to my flat when the phone rang. It was the doctor's wife from Tres Arroyos.

'Was the flight all right?' she asked. 'I had a horrible feeling that something might have gone amiss.'

In the days after that, everything seemed to be paying off at once. The last pages of the autobiography were posted to New York. A few days later, Borges received the first three copies of *El informe de Brodie* and I the galley proofs of *The Aleph and Other Stories*. The next week *The New Yorker* cabled to say they were taking the autobiography and at the same time the Brazilian Embassy contacted Borges to inform him that he had just won the biennial Inter-American Prize for Literature, also known as the Matarazzo Sobrinho Prize. *The New Yorker* paid more than $9,000 for the autobiography; the Brazilian prize, for which we had to travel to São Paulo, was $25,000.

Borges told our hosts that he did not like big hotels, so they put us up in a charming boutique establishment. We were in Brazil for a week. There were elegant dinner parties every night in the homes of rich Argentine entre-preneurs who had emigrated to São Paulo. In enormous living rooms would be a dozen round tables, each seating up to twelve people.

Señor Matarazzo had a very elegant woman who managed his social affairs. At each gathering she would place a hand on the back of what was to be Borges's chair and announce, '*O grande Borges*' – the great Borges. The words have a particular rich sound in Brazilian Portuguese, and ever after, to Borges's embarrassment, I would tease him with those words.

They wanted to fly us to Brasilia, where we could meet the president, but Borges refused the proposal. When asked what he would like to see he chose an old coffee plantation.

Back in Buenos Aires I accompanied him to the Banco do Brasil to pick up his cheque. He had no idea how much $25,000 was. To him it could have been $2,500 or even $25. It was all the same. The moment he was handed the cheque he turned and put it in my hands.

'You'd better hang on to this,' he said.

The timing of the prize had been perfect. Borges needed money for the divorce settlement. Our days were spent juggling figures and plotting strategy with the lawyers. They finally drew up a list in two columns, one headed 'Borges' and the other 'Sra de Borges'. In Borges's column was the money from the Brazilian prize, ten million pesos, and money held for him by Emecé, five and a half million. Elsa's column listed six million as her share of his Emecé earnings and nearly seven million in two properties, and a mortgage investment of another three million.

There were two additional elements to this list. One stated that she would not say or write anything against Borges, with a proviso that if she should she would incur legal sanctions. The second simply stated, 'the 3rd apartment'.

Elsa saw – or her lawyers convinced her – of the advantages to her of a divorce by mutual consent, and that's how the case was concluded.

Borges's first audience before the judge took place on 4 November 1970. He came back in a gleeful state and, with smiles and laughter, told me that the judge had spent

the court's time reading Borges's poems back to him. I
had never seen him so full of joy as he was now. Elsa was
not only out of his life, but he also never mentioned her
again. There was another and final audience before the
judge on 5 February 1971. Borges did not have to attend
and he didn't. Perhaps he had had enough of listening to
the judge read to him.

28 The Salem Mystery Solved

After I had decamped to Buenos Aires in November 1968, Vail Read and I kept in touch. I sent her Borges's books as they appeared, and she carefully charted our progress via the pages of *The New Yorker*. She and I also exchanged newsy letters.

Then, towards the end of September 1970, nearly three months after Borges had walked out on Elsa, Vail sent me a long letter to explain why John Van Dell, the Salem jeweller and Borges's friend, had found it necessary to break off relations with him back in 1967 shortly after the two couples had spent Thanksgiving Day together. For starters it was news to me that Vail and Van Dell even knew each other.

In her letter Vail announced that I was about to receive a piece of registered mail from Van Dell concerning a delicate matter that I was to communicate to Borges. In the event there was no registered letter. Instead, Vail enclosed an undated page – probably written in September – addressed by Van Dell to Borges.

Van Dell's words had been eked out with a painful struggle. He wrote on a sheet of 'Saccon Jewelers' stationery. Part of his letter was typed and part, in the middle, blanked out and then filled in by hand. Corrections were made in pencil. It was immediately apparent that Van Dell was a quite humble man who held Borges on an exalted pedestal. He began:

Dear Louis,

It is with reverence and respect that I address you in this manner. If I call you Mr. Borges, I would minimize the proud feeling I acquired through your acquaintance. This is John, John Van Dell of Salem that deserted you so abruptly because at that time it was best to do so.

Van Dell went on to say that it had been in Cambridge that 'the seeds of doubt in relation to your marriage were revealed.' He and Borges had been sitting together and after a long silence, 'with a visible preoccupied mind', Borges said, 'John, the relations between Elsa and me are cloudy, what can you do, what can I do?'

Van Dell did not answer. After another long pause, Borges repeated, 'John, you didn't answer.'

Realizing at last that Borges was 'in urgent need of a solution', Van Dell spoke to Elsa. He took her into another room and told her that she personally was responsible for the life or death of a genius and that if she did not act with proper consideration for Borges, Van Dell would disgrace her throughout Argentina.

Clearly distressed, Van Dell in his letter to Borges wrote:

> How tragic that our friendship should end through Elsa's behaviour. She would put in her pocketbook any object that, if she would have asked us, perhaps we would have been glad to give it to her. We tolerated it for a while, but this of course could not continue.

Van Dell was full of remorse for not having been able to tell Borges any of this. He considered the matter too delicate to trouble Borges with given 'the sensitive situation that existed between you and Elsa at that time, but most of all would have saddened your noble mind or damaged your frail body.'

There was a slightly different take and a less guarded approach in Vail's letter to me. On the Thanksgiving evening after they had spent the day together, Borges asked Van Dell to take a walk with him alone. 'There, with the rain streaming down his face, and weeping, Borges confided that he was nearly going out of his mind with Elsa's sexual obsessiveness and other demands . . .'

Again, Vail is more explicit about Elsa's thieving. She had been stealing small treasures from the Van Dells on every visit. For a while they tried to put up with the situation,

but when they found Elsa first in their silver and then in
Mrs Van Dell's clothes cupboard, they had to stop being
hospitable.

In a second letter from Vail, dated 29 November 1970,
she relates in more detail what Van Dell had told her:

> It was a bad marriage from the start. She was a cruel woman;
> an avaricious woman. But Borges's friends would have forgiven
> her even her taking things, whether she was a kleptomaniac,
> or just because she wanted them. What made it a terrible
> marriage was that she did not really think of Borges at all, but
> only of herself.

On that rainy Thanksgiving evening Borges revealed
that Elsa had not spoken to him for three days because
he refused to be *macho*. 'Walking in the little old cemetery
near the Van Dell house,' wrote Vail, 'Borges had pled for
help: "I am helpless! blind! Before we were married I told
her I could never have intercourse with her, because I am
impotent. And she *agreed* that we would have a platonic
marriage, because many people of our ages have platonic
marriages."'

I was long aware of Elsa's propensity for small-scale
surreptitious collecting. In restaurants and hotels, she
slipped any number of things like napkins and place mats,
match books and ashtrays – provided they were printed
with the place's logo – into her handbag. She was also fond

of those tiny jars of jams and marmalades served at hotel breakfasts. She told Borges that she planned to give a little party for her friends displaying these items round the room and wouldn't they be thrilled. She probably meant envious. But the scale of theft from friends like the Van Dells I found impossible to swallow. On the other hand, her unsatisfied sexual needs and the despair this plunged her into deserve understanding.

In the weeks following his separation, and with court proceedings soon to take place, Borges was in a fragile physical and mental state. I felt I had no choice but to spare him the story revealed in the letters from Van Dell and from Vail Read.

I never mentioned any of it to him.

When all had been definitively laid to rest, Borges made Fernández Ordóñez a handsome gift of the manuscript of one of his stories.

There had been some signs of Borges's new-found joy before the first court appearance. He was out-going, untroubled, carefree. In September he had travelled to Rosario with his mother for three days. At ninety-four, this must have been the last time she accompanied him on any of his travels. Only a few days later, he and I were off to Casilda again; this time he had invited Haydée Santillán to join us. And then a week later Borges and I were on a romp, setting up his books on their old shelves in the Maipú flat.

An amusing incident took place at this time. One afternoon as I handed over a *New Yorker* cheque to doña Leonor she showed me how clever she was with the accumulation of these dollar cheques she'd been receiving from me. In a big chest in her bedroom she opened a drawer and showed me a wad. Some of the cheques had lain there for months. I mildly chided her, saying these cheques should be deposited in a bank.

'Ah, no, *m'hijo*,' she answered. 'Don't you see that as the value of the peso keeps going down when I cash these cheques I get a better exchange.'

Borges stood by us, taking all this in.

'But if the dollars were in a bank growing in interest, when you cashed a cheque it would be worth even more.'

No, she wasn't having it. She was clever with money and at her age lent it privately for mortgages.

'But, *madre*,' Borges cut in, 'you should listen to di Giovanni; he's our friend. You're ninety-four and you don't understand what he's telling you; I'm only seventy and I understand him.'

Several months earlier, Borges had slipped off from the Library one afternoon in a hangdog mood to explain to Neil MacKay, of the British Council, why he could not travel to Oxford to accept the university's offer of an honorary doctorate. Of course, Borges had been unable to tell the truth – that he could no longer travel with Elsa – and so invented something that sounded like his health was in question. As I knew a divorce was only a few months away and that that would change the equation, I phoned MacKay for an appointment. I suggested to him that Borges's problems would soon be resolved and asked if it were possible for Oxford to renew their offer. MacKay was delighted and on the spot gave me a choice of seven different dates between the coming September and April of the next year.

I went directly back to the Library.

'Borges,' I started, 'about that Oxford degree—'

'No, no,' he cut in angrily, 'I don't want to hear another word about that. It would have been the greatest honour of my life and I had to turn it down, so let's hear no more about it.'

'But I've just come from seeing MacKay. They are happy to renew the offer any time you want to go. You can choose from seven different dates.'

He could not contain himself. He immediately hustled me along the streets to Calle Maipú. There, turning the key in the lock he rushed straight to his mother's bedroom, calling out with boyish excitement, '*Madre, madre,* di Giovanni has got me back the degree from Oxford!'

When it came down to the dates he said he would choose the last date available – 29 April 1971.

'Why that date?' I asked him. 'Why not sooner?'

'Ah,' said Borges, 'that way I'll have more time to look forward to it.'

What impressed me was the utter boyishness of his reaction, not least of which was sharing the news at once with his mother. With Borges the old attachments always won out.

The Maipú flat soon became home ground to me. When his mother went out to church on Sunday mornings, Borges would ask me to come and work with him there. By Buenos Aires standards it was quite a modest household. Six floors up on the street side of the building, the entrance door to the flat boasted a simple bronze plaque inscribed 'Borges'. Inside was a vestibule, with doña Leonor's bedroom off to the left and the living room, with a dining area at one end, off to the right. Squeezed between these two were a bathroom and Borges's room, a cell barely big enough for his single bed. The floors throughout were parquet.

Leonor slept in a small double bed, a mahogany four-poster. She would always invite me to sit beside her there and she called me '*m'hijo*' – my son. The room's French doors opened onto a narrow balcony, whose parapet was a masonry flower bed with a railing above it. She kept thorny cactus-like plants out here and though she watered them often they always seemed unkempt to me. From this eyrie, looking past the monumental 1912 Palacio Paz, since 1939 the Círculo Militar – it offered a touch of Paris with its great mansard roof – was a good view of the Plaza San Martín. Here grew tall jacarandas, whose fallen blossoms carpeted the lawns and paths below in a glorious purple-blue. José Paz, for whom the *palacio* had been named, was the founder of the daily *La Prensa*.

Leonor spent most of her time in bed, using the phone all day long to stay in touch with her friends. Fani, the maid, served meals to her here. Borges's mother ate porridge while she chattered away, and consequently the mouthpiece of the phone was always clogged and encrusted with the remnants of her breakfast.

A feature of the living room was a heavy mahogany sideboard, a family heirloom, on which was placed a silver basin that had accompanied Isidoro Suárez on his campaigns in the wars of independence. Also standing there were some old silver matés on tripod bases. On the wall over this sideboard was one of Norah Borges's paintings, a large cheerful annunciation. On other walls hung a print by Piranesi and one by his disciple Rossi, the famous Roman '*Veduta della piramide di Cestio*'. The Piranesi was a view of the Temple of Dio Canopo at Hadrian's villa in Tivoli. (These were the two Roman engravings listed for retrieval at the head of chapter 27.)

At the end of the room were a mahogany dining table on trestle legs and a set of chairs. Behind the table were the major part of the flat's bookshelves and Borges's library. Five shelves rose up from some cabinets along the floor, and at the top various objects – plates, etc. – were on display.

In low cabinets and on other shelves round the room were the massive sets of encyclopedias, in French, German, Spanish, and English, that their publishers had made gifts of to Borges over the years.

A final feature of the household was the steadfast, redoubtable maid Fani, who inhabited a tiny servant's quarters at the back of the flat. Epifanía Úveda de Robledo was her full name. She was a native speaker of Guaraní, as Borges was fond of telling everyone, and she hailed originally from the northern Province of Corrientes. She had been with Borges and his mother for years and years.

Fani adored Borges and doña Leonor and was not cowed by Borges's mother, with whom she could engage without submissiveness. Not many realized that she was illiterate. Perhaps not many realized that Fani was also a consummate eavesdropper. I often spotted her lurking and listening half-hidden behind a door jamb. I doubt that anything passed between Borges and his mother that Fani was unaware of; to my mind the accounts of Borges's affairs that she recounted after his death were both truthful and accurate.

Fani's aim in life was to protect Borges. There was an innate innocence about her that seemed to me to make it impossible for her to tell anything but the truth. She had a daughter, Stella, who had a son, and sometimes they inhabited the servant's quarters with Fani, but you never knew whether they were just visiting or spending a few days. There seemed to be a kitchen back there – and of course Fani's mops and brooms and buckets and cleaning rags. Another thing about Fani was her agelessness. She had that sallow colour typical of the Guaranis, but she always looked the same.

This then, Maipú 994 at the corner of Charcas, was the hub of Borges's world.

30 Looking Back

A library of books has been written about Borges and his literary work. Biographies, bibliographies, critical interpretations, volumes of hagiography and volumes of impious loathing, puffed-up doctoral theses, and countless interviews that tend to plough the same ground over and over. A small portion of this work may be classed as genuine scholarship with something to say, but most of it is of transient interest or less. Many of the books on Borges reveal more about their authors and their authors' cleverness than they do about Borges. This is to say nothing of the myriad of unreadable studies that proliferate in academic journals and are read by nobody.

I have found in the biographies a good deal about Borges the writer and the intricacies of his early literary days in Buenos Aires, fascinating perhaps to specialists but containing nothing about him as a man, nothing personal, nothing about his true character. While this is especially true of those researchers who came to Borges only through his work and other critics' work about him, it is also true of a handful of Argentine writers who knew him in his lifetime as friends and intimates. It is as though Borges the man were off limits, unapproachable. The present book, *Georgie & Elsa*, is unapologetically about the missing Borges who will not be found in the library.

In his fiction it cannot be denied that Borges wrote an impeccable prose. Where did it come from? It began at the side of his paternal grandmother Fanny Haslam, who was born in Staffordshire, and his 'grand-aunt Caroline'. With these two he grew up speaking English. Fanny Haslam was a great reader of the English classics; great-aunt Caroline in 1910, when Borges was eleven, presented him with a copy of Pope's translation of the Odyssey, which overwhelmed him.

Borges's prose style also had its roots in his father's passion for nineteenth-century English poetry – Keats, Shelley, and Swinburne – and his interest in books about the East by Lane, Burton, and Payne. The prose style came with Georgie's pedigree reading, or devouring, of English literature, for it may be said that Borges came to write Spanish with the prose of England. When we read a book like Conan Doyle's *Study in Scarlet* or one of those incomparable articles from the Eleventh Edition of the *Encyclopædia Britannica*, we think we are reading Borges.

In other words, he wrote Spanish while in his ear he heard English. This enabled him to trim Spanish rhetoric and bombast, to write a lean Spanish. In a way, it was all an accident of birth that he made the most of. At a time when the Argentine intelligentsia worshipped Paris and was in the grip of French culture Borges played the maverick and hewed to English.

But there is another side to Borges's writing career that is less examined. In his major work, the stories, he was slow, painstaking, and unprolific, yet at different times he also ground out – that is, wasted his time on – an inordinate amount of hackwork. Was this in frustration or dissatisfaction with himself? He wrote an appalling series of booklets, handbooks for students on a variety of subjects, each composed with a woman collaborator. He and Alicia Jurado wrote on Buddhism; he and Esther Zemborain de Torres on American literature. Borges accepted these commissions but would toss them off as jokes while he abused his collaborators with mocking accounts of what he regarded as their shortcomings.

Alicia Jurado, he told me with a laugh, was a keen Buddhist, which was not true. Borges made this up because Alicia insisted on including in their booklet certain of the main tenets of Buddhist philosophy. At the same time, she told me that Borges was frivolous and wanted only to record the rare and exotic oddities of the Buddhist creed. In the booklet written with Esther, he recounted with some glee that as a good Catholic she fought him tooth and nail against stating that Hemingway had taken his own life.

He seemed trapped in his male superiority. Victoria Ocampo was a woman he praised and thanked in print for paying for at least one of his early eye operations and later for securing him his directorship of the National Library, yet he was unable to refrain from any opportunity to belittle her behind her back. Alas, Borges had the unforgiveable clockwork habit of turning on and rejecting people he once held in high esteem. As his fame grew he did this to a whole stream of writers that he at one time had glorified to the skies – Ricardo Güiraldes, Macedonio Fernández, Evaristo Carriego, Miguel de Unamuno.

Nor was he generous with his contemporaries. As a way of cocking a snook at the literary establishment, he made a sport of praising mediocre scribblers, while he harboured resentments about the fame of real writers, about whom he expressed wilful ignorance. Saul Bellow, when he won the Nobel Prize, was dismissed with the words, 'Never heard of him.' Borges took for granted the endless help he received from friends and well-wishers, barely thanking anyone and never paying for any of it. Nobody likes owing anything to his contemporaries, he confided in his 1935 story 'The Approach to al-Mu'tasim'. It was a remark carefully sanctified by his telling us that Dr Johnson said it first.

Borges's self-deprecation, his belittling of his own work, was one of his tricks to win over the public. He cultivated a simple, frugal, spartan existence and maintained an acceptable outward stance of grinding no religious or political axe. In this respect he used his blindness for whatever end it served him. He did not read the newspapers, so felt he should be pardoned for not knowing what went on in the world. Except in literary matters, he avoided the polemical. He was canny. His bookishness and harmless out-of-the-way learning, his devotion to remote subjects like Old English and Old Norse, he relied on to exempt him from displaying any interest in the real world.

Throughout his life Borges was not untainted by various forms and degrees of posturing. He once told me the story of a young man, a protester, a political activist, who invaded his Buenos Aires university classroom and began shouting out that, for his reactionary politics, Borges was a dinosaur. The student was no doubt a Peronist. What was Borges's response? Deadly serious, he suggested the two of them step outside into the hall to settle the matter. This was the old-fashioned, gentlemanly way of fighting a duel. The very same thing happened in 1971 at Columbia University when a Puerto Rican student verbally attacked him in the lecture hall. Again Borges challenged the student to a contest out in the corridor. In neither case would these objectors have laid a finger on Borges and he doubtless knew it. He was old, frail, decrepit, and on both occasions numerous onlookers were present. What was he playing at? This was unthinking macho bluster.

Borges, an otherwise mild-mannered man, was in thrall to a glorification of violence that seems at odds with his bookishness. At the close of his story 'The South' his alter ego, a city librarian named Juan Dahlmann, is being taunted by local toughs in a country pub. When he asks what they want one of them whips out a knife and invites Dahlmann to fight with him. Dahlmann is thrown a weapon. The improbable story ends with the line, 'Dahlmann clutches the knife, which he may not know how to handle, and steps out onto the plain.' A disproportionate number of his stories end similarly, with a sudden bullet or knife thrust taking a character's life.

As for his renowned anti-Peronism, for me that too had elements of posturing about it. Perón's followers had humiliated Borges, his mother, and his sister, as they had many others of his class. Borges claims that they told him that since he had supported the Allied cause during the war, such treatment was only to be expected. This was not exactly an Argentine version of *Kristallnacht*, and abroad, in America and Europe, anti-Peronism was a soft, safe option.

In his political myopia it never occurred to Borges that it was his social class who had opened the door to Perón and was responsible for his rise to power. Argentine conservatives – or reactionaries – did nothing to lift the masses, while the Peronists came along and did. The deprived poor in Argentina were invisible to Borges and to his circle of conservatives, of whom he claimed to be one. Perón's failure was rooted in his mediocrity and his extension and glorification of that long blight on Argentina – militarism. Worst of all he failed to provide the lower classes with a true legacy, a European-style ideology based on democratic principles.

The Peronists' bankruptcy is all too evident. They represented all things to their followers, having leftist, centre-right, and right-wing factions, and consequently what could any of it have meant to anyone? In order to inject some semblance of substance into their beliefs, Perón's authoritarian movement had to invent and rally round the neologism '*Justicialismo*' – supposedly meaning, vaguely enough, a movement that promotes justice.

Borges conveniently styled himself an anarchist, a philosophical anarchist, a freethinker, in a way that was broad enough to give no offence. The true anarchist, however, has a committed social conscience and a thirst for social equality, concepts far beyond Borges's powers of interest or comprehension. Here was another example of his posturing.

What is astonishing about Borges's political views – so many of them wrong-headed and contradictory – was the fact that his anti-Peronism had brainwashed him to the point that he embraced any regime, no matter whether legitimate or illegitimate, so long as it was anti-Perón. This threw him straight into the arms of General Videla, the murderous author of the Dirty War, whose junta Borges once characterized as made up of 'gentlemen'.

Borges seemed to thrive on idiosyncrasies and arbitrariness, which ran the gamut from the ridiculous to the self-destructive. One time I accompanied him to Mar del Plata, where he delivered a talk on the Kabbalah to a Jewish society. The hosts had made the travel arrangements, as was customary, and we had tickets for return-trip flights. Mar del Plata was an hour from Buenos Aires by aeroplane. What does Borges do? After his evening lecture he announces that he does not want to fly back to the city but to take instead – as he always did in the past – the overnight coach. The organizers obliged. We travelled uncomfortably and endlessly all night. The next morning I went straight home to bed and had to give up any idea of seeing Borges later in the day at the Library. Of course, he had never asked me which means of travel I would have preferred.

At the opposite end of the scale, in later years he travelled to Chile to receive a medal from the hands of Augusto Pinochet. This was one of the worst decisions of his life. But, he maintained, in his digging-his-heels-in mode that no one was going to tell him what he could or could not do. I imagine that it never would have occurred to Borges to question and be horrified by Pinochet's well-oiled programme of eliminating Communists and other left-wingers. Borges was so universally condemned for his action that I think he came to realize his colossal mistake. But to justify it and himself, when I mentioned his folly to him, he said, 'But I thought the medal was a gift of the Chilean people.'

In the preface to his fifth book of poems, *Elogio de la*

sombra (1969), Borges wrote that 'two new themes have been added' to his old ones of mirrors, mazes, and swords. The new themes were old age and ethics. 'One of the virtues for which I prefer Protestant countries to Catholic is their regard for ethics,' he claimed. But did Borges have a true understanding of ethics – ethics as a set of moral principles? I believe his personal ethics to have been grossly deficient; I believe this book records and sets out numerous examples of these deficiencies. The ethics Borges referred to were ethics imposed by others – Protestant countries, in the particular case mentioned – and not the everyday ethics that start in one's own shoes with each sunrise. When Raúl Alfonsín won the crucial presidential election of 1983, ending eight years of military rule, Borges accepted an invitation to the Casa Rosada to meet him. The government sent a car to pick him up. When the car got to Calle Maipú there was no Borges.

One of Borges's meanest flaws was the way he used lies. His lies usually started out small enough to be passable but out of their pettiness they began to grow as he turned them over and embellished them in his head. *La calunnia è un venticello*, Rossini's barber of Seville reminds us. Because he was Borges, a writer of recognition and with a certain charisma, his lies became automatically and universally believed. He got away with this, and in the end it reached the point where, among the knots and tangles of dishonesty, he believed the lies he told.

He lied outrageously about a number of the translations he was credited with making. In his autobiography he claimed that his mother 'produced some of the translations of Melville, Virginia Woolf, and Faulkner that are considered mine.' Was this true or was he shielding himself from possible criticism? He once made me the gift of a double number of *Sur* dating from 1944 that was dedicated to contemporary American writing. In it, together with Bioy, he translated poems by John Peale Bishop, E. E. Cummings, Hart Crane, Wallace Stevens, and others, but he told me not to judge him too harshly for the translations, because in fact they had all been made by Bioy. It goes without saying that the translation he may or may not have made of Faulkner's *Wild Palms* is praised to the skies in the Argentine. It has been said of it that it is 'as good as or even better than the original.' It was another of his perversities that Borges relished the fact that his lies created confusion. Yet he himself could also be deceived by liars, often readily swallowing whatever his last speaker told him without taking the trouble to sift out their motives.

Even in his seesaw affairs with women he did himself no favours. It is said that Borges fell in love with every woman he met, provided she was good looking. How his blindness here was not a hindrance remains a mystery. His love life took place in his head. He was always either just falling in love or just being dumped by some love of his life. There was an element of continuity in this state of affairs – his love life was a cerebral business. But there was a perversity in it too. He was not averse to parading publicly a deficiency of loyalty. In a love poem written in English in 1934 he told his beloved, 'I offer you the loyalty of a man who has never been loyal.'

In the end, even his attachment to the Argentine needs examining. It is debatable whether Borges really knew Argentina. Argentina to him meant the city and environs of Buenos Aires. He proclaimed it in his travels abroad that his was a middle-class country and that he belonged to the middle class. Neither was strictly true. The city had a burgeoning middle class, who, like cliff dwellers, lived in modern towering flats. At the same time Buenos Aires had its peripheral slums, shanty towns called *villas miseria*, and its old city tenements that housed the unfortunate masses, who could hardly have been deemed middle class. But Borges knew nothing of an underclass. He belonged to that branch of the estanciero class who had come down in life and were no longer landowners. For all his declarations to the contrary, it was their narrow outlook and their aspirations that he shared.

Epilogue
Ave Atque Vale

Synecdoche. Can a marriage of only a few years' duration reveal a man's whole life? I believe this book is proof that it can.

Borges died in Geneva on 14 June 1986 and lies buried there in the Cimetière de Plainpalais under a fantasy tombstone carved with lines of Old Norse text.

The maid Fani reported in 2006 that Elsa was more than ninety years old and lived in a home for geriatrics. At the same time Fani recounted what happened on Georgie and Elsa's wedding night. Before the nuptial ceremony doña Leonor had bluntly warned Elsa that Georgie was not going to share his bed. After the wedding, when all the guests had left, Borges got ready to retire.

'Why don't you two go to the Hotel Dorá?' his mother suggested. The Dorá was not half a block away.

'No, no, and no,' insisted Borges. 'I'm staying here in my own home, in my own bed, and with my mother.'

'Poor Elsa,' Fani said, 'that night she went home alone to her own flat by bus.'

There is a vile anecdote that circulates to the effect that one day some time after his divorce Borges was walking down Calle Florida in the company of his nephew when a woman approached.

'It's me, Elsa,' the woman said.

'Who's Elsa?' Borges supposedly retorted.

The story while it contains the kind of short, sharp wit Borges aspired to (he once told me how he admired Oscar Wilde in this respect) at the same time is just too pat, too cruel. To me the incident is apocryphal; for Borges's sake I hope it's apocryphal. Surely the spark of humanity can't have been so readily extinguished in him.

In the aftermath of the divorce, when Elsa was subtly being interviewed by women's magazines for dirt on Borges, she claimed that she and he had parted friends. With regard to me, she had a bit of a field day. She said that at first she thought Georgie had left her to go back to his mother.

> Then [Elsa continued] I thought that the influence of Norman Thomas di Giovanni . . . may have damaged our marriage. He always tried to exercise control over Borges. He did not commiserate with me. Di Giovanni accompanied Georgie to the tribunal, and it was he who drew up the grounds for divorce. There was a moment when I almost had the feeling that I was

divorcing di Giovanni. For one split second I thought that it wasn't really Georgie who had separated from me.

In his hefty biography, *Georgie 1899-1930*, Alejandro Vaccaro entirely dismisses Elsa, writing that Borges's early infatuation with her 'would be irrelevant were it not for the fact that, forty years later, destiny reunited them and Elsa became his first wife.'

Looked at coldly, the marriage to Elsa was an exercise in cruelty and deception. For Borges to have linked himself so recklessly to an intellectually uninterested woman amounted to plain opportunism – maybe his, maybe his mother's – and a total abdication of common sense.

Of Elsa, what remains to be said? We know nothing of when she died or where or under what circumstances. We do not know where she lies buried. We do know that she was predeceased by her son. Contact with a member of her family – her sister Alicia's grand-daughter – provided no information except that the family had long since been out of contact with one another. In death, it seems, Elsa slipped anonymously into anonymous eternity.

For all her peccadilloes, her malice, her meanness, and her petty larceny, Elsa deserves neither blanket condemnation nor to be ground out of existence – airbrushed out of Borges's life – in a dismissive, hard-hearted fashion. After all, it was Georgie who chose her.

On Borges

Jorge Luis Borges's career as a writer of fiction was a series of paradoxes.

He had published three books of poems and five of erudite essays before trying his hand at the short story, which eventually brought him his international fame. His first efforts, mainly in a book called *A Universal History of Infamy*, consisted of sketches and borrowings from out-of-the-way sources, together with clever hoaxes and reviews of non-existent books. It was a tentative beginning, inconspicuous and roundabout. In fact, among the great writers of our time it is difficult to recall a more timorous debut. Also remarkable is the paucity of his production. His ultimate renown rests on a mere thirty-four stories, which were written between 1933 and 1953 and collected in two books, *Ficciones* (1944) and *El Aleph* (1949 and 1952).

Borges had only a handful of admirers in his native Buenos Aires until he was in his sixties, when he shared a European literary prize with Samuel Beckett. He was in his seventies when the awards and prizes and honours – among them, honorary degrees from both Oxford and Cambridge – swamped him. He never wrote a novel, and his work in Spanish and in translation was not popular (from the outset his stories were considered cryptic, puzzling, and full of abstruse concepts), but slowly he became the darling of academics the world over and to this day is read and admired by a host of other writers and by a universal literary and cultural intelligentsia.

In his later years his political and social views gained him notoriety and probably cost him a Nobel Prize.